T0068224

HALFTIME

Midlife and Midcareer Reflections
of a Johannesburg Woman

Valerie Ndou

WESTBOW
P R E S S®
A DIVISION OF THOMAS NELSON
& ZONDERVAN

WestBow Press books may be ordered through booksellers or by contacting:

WestBow Press
A Division of Thomas Nelson & Zondervan
1663 Liberty Drive
Bloomington, IN 47403
www.westbowpress.com
844-714-3454

ISBN: 978-1-6642-6111-2 (sc)
ISBN: 978-1-6642-6110-5 (hc)
ISBN: 978-1-6642-6112-9 (e)

Library of Congress Control Number: 2022905115

Print information available on the last page.

WestBow Press rev. date: 04/07/2022

CONTENTS

One Muffled Sob 1
All Pumped Up! 7
"Knowledge Speaks but Wisdom Listens" 12
Looking Back from the Future 17
The Roller Coaster 25
Living It Forward 30
All Eyes Downcast. 38
Power, Politics, and Much Ado about a Sandwich. 44
The Five Stages of Grief. .50
    Stage 1: Are You Kidding Me? 50
    Stage 2: Can Anyone Hear Me?. 55
    Stage 3: Fast and Beg. 60
    Stage 4: Baptism by Fire 66
    Stage 5: Gratitude. .69
A Small Cloud 72
Roundtable Reflections 76
Affluent Actualizing 82
Charities and Recitals. 88
A "Fishy" Proposal. 92
Going Home 96
Another Sob and Then a Sigh 101
Hope Deferred (Again) 105
A Little Piece of Paradise. 113
Tea, Talk, and Scones 117
Chasing Business (Up and Down Country) 120
Six Grounding Weeks. 126
Saying Goodbye to an Era 135

ONE MUFFLED SOB

I hate farewells. That's why I walked casually into the kitchen of the School of Business and Economics on February 28, 2017. I felt a flush of embarrassment as I realized I was late for my own farewell tea. There sat my boss and many of my colleagues in a messy circle, waiting for me. I glanced at my watch and mumbled an apology. Academics are near-perfect individuals, and I had managed to melt in with everyone else in keeping time, ensuring marks and reports were submitted on time. I had even mastered the time difference between Johannesburg and Australia, where the university's head office was based. I have spent many years kicking myself for being a few minutes late for almost everything, but I didn't feel sorry about it on this day. I felt embarrassed that I should have known better than to keep my boss waiting six whole minutes for me—and even more embarrassed that I was resigning from a job after only nine months. Okay, so it had actually been twelve months since I had begun my teaching career, but only nine of those had been on a permanent basis. I feared that I appeared very shallow and unfocused. After all, many of my colleagues had been teaching here for four to six years, and my boss had been in the same job for fourteen years.

Oh well, I thought, quickly consoling myself. I really could not afford to compare myself with anyone at this stage. After all, I didn't have much time. I was already forty-one, and I had to make the most of my remaining years. I knew I needed to make a greater impact in organizations, and the past year had proven that I could not wholeheartedly fulfill both teaching and organizational consulting desires simultaneously.

As I sat somewhat uncomfortably in the chair in the school kitchen, I wondered why I had been here in the first place. What had been the purpose of my being here such a short time, and what had I done to deserve a farewell tea and these kind words that were currently reeling off my boss's tongue? The real heroes who were rightfully deserving of honor were my colleagues who had served long and hard. They came here semester after semester, year after year, to teach the same subjects to different faces, to go through the repetitive processes of designing unit activities, setting assignments, teaching, marking and assessing, and setting exams and all the administrative pressures that accompanied these core activities.

Teaching had actually been therapeutic for me. After the war season of corporate work, it had seemed to be exactly what the doctor ordered: peaceful (on the surface), minimal interaction with mature adults, very few meetings, and sweet flextime. Of course, many of these attractions sounded much better than they felt in reality, but I really had needed a break from organizational politics, long hours, never being off-duty (my cell phone followed me everywhere I went), and being stuck in daily traffic at peak times. It had been wonderful to spend time with the next generation of working professionals, preparing them for something that neither they nor I could describe with confidence, considering the rate at which the world of work was changing.

Before I could fully immerse myself in my revelry, my boss awakened me by asking me to say a few words.

I felt a sense of relief at being asked. This was my opportunity to almost apologize for my short tenure and to assure my colleagues of my intention not only to stay in touch but to collaborate in a multitude of organizational and business initiatives.

It struck me how much less I dreaded speeches now. In fact, I secretly looked forward to them because they were opportunities to teach (which was something I would never tire of doing) as well as opportunities to challenge my vocabulary and linguistic intelligence (if there is any such thing) and to analyze whether I had grown and developed in my sophistication of vocabulary and articulation.

So very naturally and effortlessly did I begin my speech by thanking my colleagues for their time and for the many different conversations we had shared over the past twelve months. I thanked a few colleagues who had in fact become friends to me for their encouragement toward academic research and for fully infecting me with a love for research and article writing.

I had loved the culture of academia, I must admit. I had not had any official working hours, but I had lecture and consultation times, and I needed to be online to assist and respond to students at some time during the day. It had suited me well, and I had felt much less burdened than before. Unfortunately, all of these benefits had come at a price, and this was fully reflected by my pay slip. Academia just did not pay, and all my colleagues seemed to have made peace with that. To compensate for the fleeting capacity to take international holidays and shop extravagantly, they all seemed to have delved into the theoretical heaven of doctoral studies and research, which fortunately was an area I enjoyed and admired.

Back to my farewell party. I moved on in my speech to the students and was mildly surprised at the change in my voice. Real emotion came about as I joked about loving the students despite the gray hair they had brought me. I not only heard it but felt it. A deep muffled sob interrupted my speech out of the blue. I laughed out loud as I commented on how emotional the teaching experience had been for me. Then without warning or notice, the reasons for my deep emotion came tumbling out of my mouth.

I shared with my captivated audience how important it had been for me to come and teach. After years of working in organizations and living business and economics day after day, season after season, financial year after financial year, strategy after strategy, I had finally stepped out of the cycle and was standing by, reflecting on the many experiences. I guess it could be described as a form of metacognition. I really had to opt out of the cycle in order to take a deep look at what was actually going on and why people behaved the way they did.

I had totally lost control. I hated it, but I could not stop. My heart needed healing, and if that meant using these precious few moments to debrief, then so be it. I didn't care what they thought of me or how they might misconstrue my story. I was going to tell it in brief and enjoy the momentary relief that this brought me.

I tried as best I could to describe the difficult times I'd had at work without disclosing too much detail about former colleagues or associates. I spoke of the trips home during which I reflected quietly to myself and marveled at not only the state of the organization but also the extent to which humans were capable of corrupting self and others without so much as a second thought.

I recalled the difficult conversations that had taken place in the boardroom when I had refused to back down, either due to my insistence on standing up for what was right or when I was simply selling my vision for what the organization might become with a little less self-centeredness by the leaders.

And the moral of the story was that everything matters. How you respond and act at work matters. When you bury your head in the sand and allow evil to prevail, it does. When you chip into a conversation and add a small but negative comment about someone who is not present to defend him- or herself, it all matters.

There, I had said it! I had finally allowed myself to vent and release some of the pressure I had been bottling up since leaving my executive job eighteen months ago. I felt a weight lifting from my chest. I tried my best to laugh off the seriousness of my speech and hoped that no one noticed the depth from which it came. "I really need to write a book about these things!" I laughed before pleading with my audience not to hold me to account. After all, writing a book was one of those tasks that I had seen many people venture into and many fewer emerge victorious from. I had heard over and over again about writer's block, and I had been schooled enough to know that could last anywhere from two weeks to twenty years!

At the end of my speech, my mind returned to the school kitchen. *Wow, so this is the reason I was here.* I almost felt sorry for the students. Had I been too intense for them? Had I frightened them? I certainly hoped not. I ended my speech by sharing that I secretly wished someone would have shared some of these insights with me when I began my internship fifteen years earlier. Organizations were not an easy place to work and grow. That's what we do in organizations—we work, and we grow. We grow by observing other people and how they handle situations. We grow by deciding how we want to handle situations, by trying various approaches, getting our fingers burnt, and changing. We grow by deciding who becomes our role model and, in turn, deciding to be (or not to be) role models. That was the basis for my deep-rooted commitment to the students. Yes, I had said this to my audience—I loved the students, and my hope was that my presence and influence in their lives would enable them to be better employees, inspiring leaders, and ethical directors and governors one day.

I guess I felt somewhat like a grandparent looking over a young grandchild. How difficult it must be to know so much about the world that a little one is growing up in and not be able to fully express this to the child—not because of a lack of desire to school and guide, but simply due to the reality that there are no words that the loving grandparent can use to adequately describe this world that the child can fully comprehend and appreciate at this tender age. And I guess the fear that lies in the heart of the grandparent is "I may not be with you when you come face-to-face with these things. Hear and catch my heart now, while the pain of my wounds is still raw, and the passion of my resolve burns hottest."

That was the reason for that one muffled sob, the sob that I didn't know was there until it escaped mid-speech, the one sob that has given me the courage to finally write this book.

ALL PUMPED UP!

Have you ever had that feeling where you're ready for anything? You're on top of the world because you believe you are in your best shape intellectually, and you have an exciting new challenge for your newly sharpened strategic thinking capability.

Yes, you know it. It's a feeling that no one else has more insight or foresight than you, and you are not going to shy away from displaying your prowess and enlightening the masses.

I remember it quite clearly. I had just moved from a corporate position (with the flattery of having been headhunted) and was now line manager for a new unit whose focus was on monitoring and reporting on organizational data with the strategic intent of identifying bottlenecks and making recommendations for enhanced organizational efficiency.

One of my key outcomes was the internal quarterly management meeting in which all of the organization's managers came together to discuss performance data from across every business area.

It was my job not only to have collated and cleaned this data, but also to have analyzed it in order to accurately reflect progress toward strategic objectives and lead the discussion on performance improvement. I was extremely excited about my new job. I felt like I was on top of my game and had used my corporate experience well to gain insight into various areas of people development and performance improvement.

Reporting to me in my new role was an analyst, a young lady who had been working for the company for more than four years. While she was welcoming and helpful in inducting me into the role, she also appeared undermotivated and somewhat demoralized by the challenges of the role. I was fully committed to changing her tune and turning the organization's results around quickly. That is something I had admired about the corporate world. The commitment to working quickly and getting quick wins.

While I did feel like just a cog in a wheel many times, I had had the privilege of observing the leadership practices of top senior executives at my previous job. There was a culture among leaders of acting quickly and decisively, and I was adamant to implement my newly learned lessons effectively.

Leading up to the management meeting, my analyst had to collect and collate all performance information from the various departments and provide cleaned data for me to work with prior to the meeting. That sounded feasible and quite frankly rather simple.

I checked up on her day in and day out, and as we drew closer to the meeting date, I noticed that the number of excuses she was receiving from function managers (for why they had not submitted information) was growing. She complained that they "always do this" and seemed really negative about her role and the work she and I were responsible for. I really didn't believe it could be so bad. I asked her to send me a list of the managers who had not submitted information so that I could follow up with them myself. I sent out a polite but serious email to each and every defaulting manager indicating the implications of their outstanding data. I received a few responses (more apologies and excuses) and very little data. Growing somewhat fearful as the days flew by, I finally found myself in the position that I had begun to dread. It was the day before the quarterly management meeting, and there were numerous holes in the data.

I frantically began the task of visiting managers face-to-face and coming short of demanding the data. I really could not understand how this company operated. Was nobody accountable for anything? What measures were in place to ensure that people delivered on their contractual obligations?

Eventually, I received the data: books and books of Excel spreadsheets with uncleaned data. Because it was the day before the meeting, there was no time for me to let my analyst go through it. I had the unenviable task of sitting that night with the data, collating, cleaning, and analyzing. It was past 11:00 p.m. by the time I finally had a good enough set of data to actually begin my analysis.

Fortunately, I was finished by 8:00 a.m. on the day of the meeting, and the meeting itself would begin at 10:00 a.m., which gave me time to order my thoughts and prepare my presentation.

Arriving in the meeting room, I felt well prepared and proud of myself for having saved the day by pulling an all-nighter. I must say I felt very comfortable in the front of the room. This was my opportunity to prove to the CEO that he had been right to headhunt me and that I was going to be an asset to the company.

The meeting eventually began, and as I started reporting performance across the various strategic areas, the murmurs in the audience grew louder. There were at least two other people speaking at the same time, making verbal corrections to the data I was presenting! I felt a steady stream of heat rise up from my shoulders all the way to my neck and face. What? I had spoken face-to-face with each and every one of these managers, and they had personally sent me the data that had kept me awake almost all of the previous night. How could they be suggesting that these figures were incorrect and volunteering new sets of additional data now? I caught the glance of my analyst. Her eyes seemed to say to me, "I told you so," though not in a vengeful way. She seemed to have found the justification for her prior negativity and complaints.

Before long the whole meeting had erupted into a free-for-all session of numbers and information being flung about. My analyst grabbed her pen and began to make additions. We didn't even have the evidence for the numbers that were flying about, but managers and supervisors alike were making claims for better performance figures than those that were on my screen. I had never seen anything quite like it. It looked like a circus!

Did these people honestly not know the importance of this role? Organizational performance was under the spotlight for government and parastatals and was the cause of much political debate. No wonder! If this was how seriously managers of parastatals judged their own performance, then it was no wonder there were endless criticisms by opposition parties and civil groups.

With my planned presentation now quite firmly on its head, I instructed my analyst to stop taking note of all the verbal claims. I managed to calm myself and made peace with the fact that my first meeting was not going to be the splendid success I had hoped it would be. Feeling somewhat dejected and disillusioned about my new job, I gathered my sheets of paper and exhaled before gathering enough courage to address these managers.

I'm not sure how long I spoke for, but I believe my message was clear. Emphasizing the crucial importance of credible performance information, I pleaded with the managers to submit data in a timely manner, accompanied by evidence; I concluded my speech and sat down. My new boss, who appeared largely unmoved by the recent circus, reemphasized my appeals and closed the meeting. He had a knowing smile on his face that seemed to say, "Welcome to the circus!"

Wow, what could I have done differently? I guess one can never overestimate the importance of listening and reading between the lines. My analyst had dropped hints, and my observation of the managers' behavior had pointed toward a state of chaos. But my pumped-up determination had soon become puffed-up arrogance. I had believed I could do anything and ignored the undercurrents of this new organizational culture. Had I taken the time to sit with my analyst and listen to and acknowledge her concerns, I would have been better prepared for what awaited me that day.

I guess we live and we learn. Nothing is accomplished without accountability. That very week, I drew up the rule book and developed the internal policies that were to govern performance monitoring. My analyst was responsible for chasing up data two weeks prior to the next meeting and copying me on these email requests. Defaulting managers received an email and subsequently a face-to-face visit from me, and their line managers were informed of their outstanding data. Clean data sets were to be sent to me five days prior to the meeting, which would give me sufficient business hours to analyze, interpret, and prepare the report. Finally, my complete report was circulated one day prior to the meeting, and no additional data was accepted without accompanying evidence. Discussions in the meeting were focused on ways to minimize and eradicate bottleneck areas rather than on adding to presented information. Eventually, the chaotic claims of additional data died down, and an air of managerial focus and dignity was restored.

None of this was achieved overnight. It literally took months to get it right. I learned that when I'm all pumped up, I tend to over-focus on the signal and ignore the noise. But you can't afford to ignore the noise because its effect on the signal is always interference. As I learned from experience, very little can be accomplished with constant interference.

"KNOWLEDGE SPEAKS BUT WISDOM LISTENS"

The power of silence is a lesson I learned much too late in my life. I cringe when I think back at all the times that I verbally "asserted" myself in meetings and either spoke out of turn or went on for far too long as I felt the pressure to either display my knowledge (as I thought a good manager should) or demonstrate my ability to take control of a situation.

After joining a new company in 2012, I was made responsible for stakeholder interaction, which included meeting regularly with officials from government. As our first meeting began, one of my new team members introduced me to the government officials, explaining that I was the new manager responsible for organizational performance reporting.

Almost immediately, I felt what seemed to be overwhelming pressure to appear knowledgeable and to reassure the meeting's participants that I was capable of delivering in this important role. The officials embarked on an elaborate welcome, which was followed by a lengthy report on the information that had been submitted by the organization in the previous financial year. As I listened to the official providing his report, it became clear to me that the department had misunderstood and misinterpreted the organization's report. Feeling a mixed sense of excitement and anticipation at the opportunity to demonstrate my insight,

I felt my heart beating loudly in my chest as I waited impatiently for an opening in the official's speech. Nothing else mattered at that point besides my overwhelming urge to show myself competent. I noticed that a number of staff members had raised their hands, and I was sure they had the same intention—to correct the government official. But I really could not afford to let that happen. Here was a clear opportunity to prove to my audience (as well as to myself) that I was indeed the correct appointment for this important position, and what better way than to provide some much-needed correction and guidance in the very first meeting?

My hand shot up, and I verbalized my need to interject. The official delivering the speech graciously paused to allow me a chance to speak. Here it was, and I gave it my all. I organized my thoughts and articulated my concerns while pointing out the errors. There were a few nods around the room, but my colleagues still appeared desperate to make their point. The next speaker thanked me for my comments and indicated that the problem had existed for years and then explained the steps that had recently been taken in an attempt to correct the situation. I felt a warm rush of blood move from my neck up toward my face. I believe this is what "blushing" means (so black girls do blush after all). In my desperate efforts to appear competent and insightful, I had merely told the meeting what it had known for years, rather than allowing a colleague with more organizational experience and memory to respond to the government officials with a more current update. My heart was racing again, this time out of sheer embarrassment at my forwardness. How had I convinced myself that was appropriate? What a major indiscretion for the introvert that I am! It took me a few weeks to get over it.

So that was just one instance in which I inappropriately asserted myself, rather than taking a position of humility, listening and seeking to understand. Looking back, I have wondered many times why I felt the need to behave as I did in these situations. When I honestly reflect upon it, I realize that I felt an overwhelming need to prove to myself and others that I was capable. Why was that so important for me, and why could I not allow my work to speak for itself over time?

Fast-forward a few years, and I was in a coaching training workshop with a group of fellow CEOs who also were undergoing coaching training. Our master coach and trainer, Mike Cerff, was about to close the training session for the day and asked the executives to stand up for what he called a "life-changing" exercise. Mike asked us to close our eyes and repeat a vow after him. The entire post-lunch session had been focused on effective questioning and silence. Mike had demonstrated a full forty-five-minute coaching session with one volunteer from our CEO group. Watching the interaction had been quite intriguing. As a coach, Mike had facilitated the conversation, but the coachee had owned the session and had used the silence to reflect before picking up on the conversation. Now here we were on our feet, making a vow never to ask any question that we did not believe was organic and absolutely central for the benefit of the client.

This was such an incredibly meaningful moment for me. In essence, I was taking a vow never to say anything out of pressure to fill the silence, appear knowledgeable, or avoid an awkward moment. The significance of that moment for me extended way beyond coaching relationships to every single interaction, including business and personal conversations. Practically, this means that I have committed myself to level-three listening, in which I am alert to the speaker's words, gestures, and body language as opposed to allowing my mind to wander and formulating my response while they speak. In addition, this commitment means that I can rest in the assurance that I am and remain confident and capable despite the presence of silence in the conversation. I have come to perceive silence as an opportunity for reflection on the part of both the speaker and the listener. This is something that is all too often lost when we feel pressured to fill the silence with any words or comments that come to mind at the time.

Once I began to approach interpersonal interactions in a more relaxed way, it became easier to listen deeply, and I found I learned a lot more about people through listening rather than speaking. I guess we do truly live and learn.

Knowing when to be silent was an important lesson. But another difficult lesson involved knowing when to speak up and actually having the courage to follow through with one's resolve. I learned this the hard way through events that reminded me of a television series that had recently come onto the circuit. Consisting of a strip of dramatic episodes based on real-life events, this series featured mini stories with one common thread. There was always more to the story than what was initially portrayed by surface events. All of the mini dramas contained a twist that became apparent only at the end and left the audience either hanging or completely incredulous.

For me, it all began with a board resolution to investigate a senior leader for fraud and corruption. There it was. The investigation was to be launched within the next few days and carried out by an investigator who would be appointed by the board. My role was to ensure, along with another colleague, that the investigator was provided with all of the internal documents he required to carry out an independent and confidential inquiry into the allegations that had been received by the board. How difficult could that be?

I guess those have been the famous last words of other unassuming executives like myself.

The atmosphere in the office was tense over the next few days. What would happen if the leader in question got wind of the investigation? We had to do everything within our power to ensure that our conversations pertaining to the inquiry were as hushed and discreet as possible and that we facilitated a smooth and hopefully quick investigation.

By the third day, rumor had it that the cat was out of the bag and that the leader had confronted a junior manager demanding answers. Being unsure of how much of that was true, I continued to keep a straight face and pray for the best.

It was an ordinary Wednesday afternoon in the office. There were very few executives in the building at the time, and one of my staff members burst into my office to inform me that our investigator was in the building! We were all high on adrenaline and hoped that the gentleman would collect the required documentation and exit the building before arousing unnecessary suspicion.

The events that followed on that afternoon taught me a serious life lesson. Nothing is ever what it seems. I finally surrendered to the possibility that I might still be quite naive, as disturbing as that was for me. The long and short of that afternoon's events is that the contracted investigator and the leader in question were actually friends, and the motive of the contracted investigator was simply to alert the leader to the scope of the investigation to help him cover his tail and prevent dismissal. I honestly felt like an inexperienced child that afternoon. Was there ever any way of doing the right thing? Was it this easy for people to worm themselves out of consequence at all costs?

As I sat back in my swivel chair at the end of that workday, I stared at the wall. It seemed to whisper to me, "Welcome to the world, Valerie. Welcome to the world."

LOOKING BACK FROM THE FUTURE

Life can only be understood backwards;
but it must be lived forward.
—Soren Kierkegaard

Like many, I've often marveled in hindsight at the extent of what I've been gifted. Many times, I have looked back upon various seasons of my life, both personal and professional, and wondered at the growth opportunities that were placed along my path, including potential friendships, divine appointments, and second chances. However, almost all of these had one thing in common. They all came disguised as hard work, inconvenience, a setback, or an unenviable chore.

I guess hindsight really is twenty-twenty. When I stand in the present and look back upon each of these seasons, I can't imagine how I could have gotten here without the lessons learned, the relationships, the character, and the discipline that came with each season.

It took some time before I began to really get this. What if I could stand in the future and look back? What is the significance of my current overwhelmingly challenging managerial role, the "career setback" I'm opting for by staying at home with the kids, the seemingly fruitless sacrifices of cutting down on sugar and pounding the pavement while the rest of the world enjoys death by chocolate and sleeps in?

It took more than a decade of missed opportunities, but I finally learned the lesson, and of course, hindsight revealed it to me.

There's a story that I share with many friends, colleagues, and coaching clients. The emotions of the story have kept it clear and vivid, eliminating any possibility of my ever forgetting it.

Growing up in Africa, I grew accustomed to hearing my mother's friends and the elderly making statements like "I didn't sleep a wink last night!" In all of those years, I could never understand why these women felt the need to exaggerate to such extremes! I mean, I could live with "I was up for most of the night" or "I tossed and turned most of the night," but being up the entire night just seemed like an unnecessary exaggeration.

So you can imagine that when I share my own experiences of being up the entire night, I go to great lengths to convince my listeners that this language is by no means intended to be figurative; when I say this, it means I literally spent the entire night wide-eyed and sleepless.

My first full sleepless night was in August 2012. My husband had been talked into a visit to the Durban coast by a colleague who was selling an apartment by the sea. At the time, he felt it could be a great opportunity, and I tried (unsuccessfully) to talk him out of the idea because I had recently changed my working hours and was on a half-day working arrangement with reduced pay. Nonetheless, we decided to take the Durban trip anyway and have a holiday with the children since they were off school for a few weeks. With a packed car and a very excited seven-year-old son and five-year-old daughter, we stopped over at Harrismith, which was halfway between Johannesburg and Durban. It was time for lunch, and we enjoyed a hearty meal at one of the restaurants before getting back into the car to proceed with our journey. It was at that moment that I decided to check my phone briefly and found a flood of messages and an email from work announcing my boss's resignation. My heart skipped a beat. I was speechless! I really don't remember why I felt so nervous; it may have been a combination of the fact that I'd gotten along so well with this man and the knowledge that he had supported my request for reduced working hours in the face of opposition from other managers. I felt a sense of panic as my racing mind began to conceptualize the look and feel of work without my boss, and then the real cause of my stress finally hit me like a hard kick in the gut! Who was going to be our new boss? My heart was racing, and I could feel a strange pressure in my head. And there it was. I could see the problem, clear as crystal. There was a strong possibility that I could be our new boss! A new wave of panic came over me, and I began to feel nauseous. I was in no position to take on a new role, especially not an executive role. I tried to stay as calm as possible but felt even worse as I scrolled through my messages to find notes from friends and colleagues in the office who were convinced this was a wonderful opportunity for me.

I finally consoled myself with the reminder that everything took time at work. The board would have to meet and decide what was to be done, and that alone could take a few weeks. In addition, executive notice was often at least three months, so he was going to be around for at least another few months, and my life could continue as normal.

We arrived in Durban early that evening and settled into the apartment. I felt extremely unsettled internally, and I couldn't ignore the nagging feeling of being lost and confused. To add intensity to the problem, my boss phoned me to officially inform me of his resignation and ask me whether I would be keen on "acting" in the position for a few months while the recruitment process was in progress. Then he added, "You would have to come back to a full working day, though."

I felt a sense of disgust. I had changed my working hours to be more present for my children, and my son was currently in occupational therapy to help his upper-body strength and his handwriting. This was a commitment that my husband and I had made, and we had been happy to sacrifice the salary in order to make the investment in our children. I was disgusted at the mere suggestion of trading that for money. I was quick to respond. "I'm sorry, I won't be able to do that." I was proud of myself. No, I had not checked with Steven, but I was confident that we were on the same page on this one. I felt a sense of relief as soon as I said no, and my boss ended the conversation by asking me if we could chat about it once I was back in the office. I felt a dampening of my courage at this request, and in retrospect, that seems to have set the stage for my sleepless night.

When I got off the telephone, I chatted nonstop to my husband about the proposal, and he quietly listened until I was done. "Maybe this is a blessing and the break you need in your career," he said.

I felt angry and betrayed! Didn't he see how much our children needed us at the moment? Was he really willing to trade the well-being of our family for money and stature? I argued bitterly with him and accused him of focusing on the wrong things. He backed down, and I retired to bed very early that evening. However, I was awake all night long. My conversation with my boss replayed in my mind like a broken record. I must admit, I felt a sense of pride at even being considered for an executive position. They obviously felt I was capable, and that was a compliment. Had this opportunity come a few years earlier, before the children, we would have been rejoicing. But I had a much more important calling now, and I wasn't about to let anyone steal that from me!

In a nutshell, the news spoiled the rest of my trip to the coast. I felt nervous, and endless thoughts streamed through my mind. I knew I was the best-performing manager on my team at the time, and to be quite honest, I had always dreamed of being recognized for my performance and would have been excited about a promotion at any other time. Just not now, not when I had just begun working reduced hours and gotten into a successful routine with the children. Not when I could now see the results of my increased home presence. I could see it in my son's eyes. He was much less anxious and was visibly thriving. My daughter (an honest communicator) had told me how wonderful it was that I could finish my work and come and pick her up from her classroom when she was done with her work for the day. You see, previously, I had tried a number of options, like any mother would. I had been down the road of hiring another mom to collect my children and take them home, and then I would rush out of the office as soon as the clock struck four thirty to get home in time to spend some time with them before supper and bedtime.

Sleepless night number two came almost eighteen months later. Prior to that, I had turned down the acting proposal amid many discussions in private meetings and what appeared to be resentment from the powers that be. I felt as though I had been seen as turning down the call to service by the company and that I had let down the team. Nonetheless, I remained convinced that I had made the right decision and threw all my energy into packing my work into a half day and getting home to another life with the children. This was my life for another year before yet another curveball swung my way.

The date was December 20, 2013. After walking aimlessly about Sandton City mall for two hours, I finally dragged myself to my car and drove home on autopilot. I felt like a zombie. My body felt heavy and exhausted, my heart was equally heavy, and my mind was blank. Day dreaming was the only way I could cope with the anxiety I was feeling. As I arrived home, my children came running toward me to give me my daily dose of hugs and cuddles. They were six and eight years old at the time.

I made my way to our bedroom, where my husband was strewn on the bed, reading the news on his cell phone screen. As soon as I shut the door, I finally had the privacy to let out all of the emotions and stress that I had been bottling up since midday. I kicked off my work heels and let out a series of sobs. Needless to say, my husband was rather taken aback by what appeared to be a dramatic entrée. To avoid having to explain myself, I reached into my handbag and withdrew the cause of my pain and agony.

He paged through the contract of employment until he found the remuneration section. He sighed, turned toward me, and looked even more confused. "You're going to be earning a seven-figure salary!" he proclaimed. "Why are you crying?"

Those words hit me like a dagger in the chest. I had finally done it, I thought—traded the highest calling of all (motherhood) for a hefty paycheck!

I was inconsolable. Hot tears streamed down my cheeks from that time on, right through the night. I couldn't eat, and I couldn't think about anything apart from the contract of abandonment that I had signed that afternoon. All night long, I mulled over my gloomy situation. How had I gotten here? And more importantly, how had I not seen this coming?

After refusing the initial call to act in my previous boss's position, I had received another request from the CEO, a year after my boss's resignation. He had explained that he needed me to stand in the role while the recruitment process was being finalized. I had finally agreed to act in his role while the organization sought out a replacement. During my "acting" period, however, it had dawned upon me (and the CEO apparently) that I had what it took to fulfill the requirements of the role and in fact to grow and develop it significantly. I had secretly enjoyed the challenge of operating at the executive level, liaising with the governing board, and being involved in decision-making at a strategic level.

I never would have guessed that I would actually love my new corporate dress code and thrive on solving the numerous organizational complexities that seemed to rear their heads frequently in management meetings.

However, I was not to be deterred. My family meant the

world to me, and I was not willing to trade them for an executive position, no matter what the title or the price!

So you may be wondering why I applied for the permanent position (yes, I actually did apply) when it was advertised. I suddenly have recollections of Lady Macbeth asking, "Was the hope drunk wherein you dressed yourself?" Looking back, I really cannot explain in any other terms why I would have applied for the job, considering my strong convictions. The only feasible explanation is that deep inside of me, I knew I could do this job; not only was I convinced of my competence, but I also suddenly felt that I owed it to myself, my team, and my organization to take on the mantle and give it one good shot—one good shot at leading effectively and changing the culture of the organization rather than complaining about it. It was now or never because I finally had something that I'd never had before: a significant amount of influence, the type of influence you have only at the executive level. And I wasn't willing to walk away. So that's how I applied for the job.

You may be wondering at this point why I cried through that night of December 20. Well, you see, I may be skilled and competent and even highly determined, but I am also human, and I was going to try my very best to have my cake and eat it too.

I had read about women who lived their lives juggling and balancing. They seemed to enviably hold up various roles and appeared to be quite successful. I could do the same, and I was willing to give it my best. All I had to do was convince my new boss that I could work half the day and still fulfill my executive responsibilities. I was more than happy to take a pay cut, but I wanted to show him that I could do a great job and still actively parent my children.

During the selection process, I was interviewed and had to undergo numerous psychometric tests that were part and parcel of the recruitment process. I was then informed that I was the successful candidate, and a new contract of employment would be issued to me. I had planned at this point to inform the CEO of my intention to work half the day and to put my all into my job. I had worked reduced hours before and had made it work. What could be so different about this situation?

I guess the value of managing one's expectations can never be overstated. To cut a long story short, my boss could not and would not catch my vision, and that is how I came to sign the dreaded contract.

Looking back to December 20, I can still feel the overwhelming sense of hopelessness and defeat that weighed me down as I drove home that day. The fear and panic that kept me awake throughout the entire night are still very real when I think back to that night; however, I cannot imagine where I would be today had I not signed the dreaded contract of abandonment.

The truth of that situation played itself out when I finally began to work in my new role, from January 2014. My children did not have me at home by lunchtime every day, and I was not able to watch many soccer matches or music recitals for those two years, but I most certainly did not miss out on everything. As tiring and challenging as my life was during that season, I was able to schedule once-a-week "reading mom" duty for my son's grade 3 class as well as eisteddfod performances and even a number of playdates. Of course, no part of this balancing act materialized without a significant degree of drama and maniac-like driving, but it happened nonetheless.

My season as a busy executive not only developed my capabilities in strategic thinking and foresight; it also grew my confidence in leading, my courage in questioning and disagreeing, and my competence in negotiating wins for my organization, my team, and myself.

In addition, the seven-figure salary went a mighty long way toward building up our savings, investing for the future, and paying for piano, violin, and soccer lessons!

As the wise say, nothing is ever wasted.

THE ROLLER COASTER

Although I enjoyed much of my executive experience and the seemingly never-ending adventures that characterized that time, I am really grateful that I made it through that phase in one piece. A few weeks ago, I had the privilege of being invited as guest speaker by a friend who was hosting ladies' tea and talk. She interviewed me, and I got a chance to speak very briefly on various aspects of working, mothering, and studying part-time on top of working toward a fulfilling marriage. Phew! It felt like such a handful as I reflected upon this time of my life. At the same time, I felt like much less of a hero upon hearing the stories of other women who had lived through similar seasons. It was wonderful to compare stories of how we had survived the varying events during those periods, some of which were eerily similar and others refreshingly different.

After the official talk was done, some of us stayed and chatted happily about rushed seasons that involved not only pressurized deadlines and stalemates with other executives and board members but also arriving late for school activities and driving like a maniac both on the highway and along neighborhood roads while trying to arrive in time for piano lessons, vocal coaching, drama eisteddfods, you name it.

What really struck me was the similarity of the demands that seemed to be upon working mothers and the various strategies that we had all utilized to keep us somewhere on the right side of sanity and productivity in our relentless efforts to have it all. I remember one annual general meeting that was booked at a hotel near the airport. It was scheduled to begin at 10:00 a.m. and be over by 1:00 p.m. In my diary was another important appointment at the National Eisteddfod Association, where my daughter was scheduled to perform three songs in three different categories during the quarterfinal round. She had to be at the venue by 2:45 p.m. in preparation for a 3:00 p.m. start.

The annual meeting began late as stakeholders slowly streamed into the hotel almost an hour later than scheduled. By some form of miracle, I managed to leave the event at 2:00 p.m. (only because I skipped lunch) and began the rough journey to collect the children from school.

I was driving at a minimum speed of 140 kilometers per hour, praying that I wouldn't meet any traffic cops and that there would be no traffic jams. (Is there grace for moments like that?) Once the kids had been collected, there was a flurry of activity in the car as my daughter changed out of her school uniform and into her pretty performance dress. Facecloths and baby oil were strewn all over the seat, and she was dutifully warming up her voice while she got on with it, with a little help from her brother.

I pulled up to the eisteddfod venue, parking the car completely outside the parking lines, but all that mattered to us was that we had made it. My little girl sang her very best, and she walked away with an excellent set of results on all three of her performances. My heart was full, but I was exhausted. I could feel the adrenaline subsiding, which made me feel ready for bed at just 5:00 p.m. *Surely, one cannot live like this forever!* I thought.

I laughed to myself as I drove home from my friend's tea-and-talk morning. She had shared with me how she had come close to many an accident, rushing to collect children from aftercare or shipping kids from one extramural to the other. I could fully relate. I remembered a day when I had rushed out of the office in order to collect both my son and daughter and take them to their piano lesson at the home of a retired teacher. The teacher came highly recommended, and I was intent on providing only the best for my children. Because I was running late (once again), I had to defy the speed limit and stepped fully on the gas of my 4x4 in my quest to get to the school in double-quick time. Taking the off-ramp from the highway, I navigated my way to the right lane of a major road as nimbly as possible, in preparation for my upcoming right turn. I made it! Feeling encouraged, I continued on my fast lane to the school and noticed a green light that was likely to turn amber as I crossed the intersection. I was sure I could make it through easily, and there was no turning traffic on the opposite side of the road. As I sped toward the intersection, I noticed a small passenger car approaching the traffic light and was horrified to notice that it wasn't stopping! The smaller car crossed the intersection seconds before I arrived at the same spot, and in my panic to avoid the car, I swung to the right, climbed the bank, and missed the traffic light pole by inches.

You would think I would have slammed on the brakes at this juncture and stopped the car. I didn't. I could not afford to stop because time was ticking. I had to turn into another street soon thereafter, and it was only then that it landed with me: I could have died in that spot! I had caught a glimpse of another car waiting at that intersection, and a lady inside it had gasped as she watched me miss not only the smaller car but also the pole. What was I doing, and where was my life going?

Of course, there was no time to ponder and reflect. What mattered then was that we all managed to get to piano lessons safely, and I was satisfied over honoring the appointment and making another valuable investment in the lives of the children.

Looking back on that day, I shiver at that moment of recklessness. How was I living?

Another memory came to mind as I reflected upon that season. This time I had a board meeting that was scheduled to end by 5:00 p.m. I had optimistically informed the music teacher that I would collect the children at 5:30 p.m. from her home. I was fully organized upon entering the meeting, sure that this would help me get out of the office promptly after the meeting. Oh, what self-deception!

The meeting began on time, and I felt cheerfully expectant that there would be no difficult issues to cause time delays, which often occurred as members disagreed and proposed new ideas, and then others did the same, resulting in wasted time and no resolutions. Somewhere along the way, however, there was a considerable delay, and I remember looking down at my watch and noticing that it was five o'clock, and we were nowhere near the end of the agenda. I could feel the stress coming on and began to feel a premature sense of sympathy for the children. They were going to finish their lessons and have to wait for me to get there. I was still hopeful, though. I hoped we could get through the other agenda items quickly so I could be on my way in no time. The next time I looked at my wristwatch, it was twenty minutes past five. How incredibly quickly time had flown. With my heart racing and, I'm sure, a clearly irritated look on my face, I reached out for my cell phone and sent a text to the music teacher. I apologized that I was running late and told her that I expected to be there at approximately six thirty. Once I received her reassuring response, I relaxed and could now focus on the remaining proceedings of the meeting.

To cut a long story short, the meeting ended at six, and I pulled up to the music teacher's gate at 6:45 p.m. I felt like an awful mother and scolded myself for not having arranged transport home for the children, which would have avoided this. As always, the children were happy to see me and jumped cheerfully into the car, exclaiming how cold and hungry they were. I asked them where they had been waiting, and my son explained that the music teacher had told them to play in the garden while she and her husband ate supper. I gasped! Who does that—who leaves two small children, all of nine and seven years old, out in the cold while she eats her dinner? I was clearly offended but silently accepted the blame for not planning better. This was hard. How do you successfully do professional life as well as parenting without killing yourself or your children?

The upside of this mad season lay in the financial benefits of working in senior management. When that text message came in from the bank on the twenty-fifth of every month, it somehow helped me forget about the difficulties that the season brought. I had been very surprised at how handsome the remuneration and benefits were at this level, and I remember trying hard to use up my monthly cell phone allowance, which I never quite succeeded at. I remember hundreds of rands' worth of airtime and data rolling over month after month, not to mention the fact that I could fill my car up twice in the month with the fuel allowance provided. This really was the life when you were not rushing around like mad. For the first time in a long time, money was not an issue, and my longing was beginning to shift to more time. I had money now, but there really was very little time to spend it on anything. Weekends were never long enough, and it was difficult to find a suitable time to take annual leave. So to some degree I was "cash Mommy," who could afford almost anything the children asked for, but for whom time was really scarce. I privately joked about having money and no time to spend it.

Moreover, work was getting challenging, not because of the amount of work that needed to be done, but because of the human resources and governance problems that seemed to arise one after the other. I had a vision for the organization, but things were taking an unwanted and certainly unexpected turn. This felt like nothing I had signed up for, and I wanted to change things to make it an organization I could be proud of. Unfortunately, there weren't very many who shared my vision.

LIVING IT FORWARD

S o it's all well and good to be able to look back with twenty-twenty vision and gain the insight that shows us the why and the worth of our past experience.

But as I mature in both age and character, I make a conscious effort to learn from my daily experiences. If I later look back on today, what perspective will I wish I had had concerning my current circumstances, and which opportunities will I kick myself for not taking hold of with both hands?

Having just read Malcom Gladwell's *Outliers*, I am vividly aware of the circumstances and blessings of history that have enabled me to be here, in Johannesburg in 2017, with two masters' degrees, a thriving middle-class family, a rich catalog of work experience, and the privilege of being coached regularly. I was alive to the clear and present opportunity of today. I am not the first Sandton mother to leave formal employment to work from home. But I am indeed one of few mothers with an opportunity to employ my skills to self-enterprise and, above all, with an opportunity to sit and reflect and indeed write a book.

In comparison, though, sitting here and reflecting on the past is so much easier than deciding on how to intentionally and purposefully put today to good use, employing my time and energy toward tomorrow's success. I would, quite frankly, much rather deconstruct and micro-analyze yesterday.

But how do I really live it forward when it's so difficult to identify the actual opportunity of today? Particularly when it almost always seems as though I am chasing my own tail from hour to hour, to get to the unending tasks that must all be completed today? It seems as though I spend most of my time driving and sitting in traffic rather than focusing on my priorities.

I've found it works when I time-travel to another point on my timeline. For example, five years from now, how will my life be different from what it is today, and what will I miss about the situation I am in currently?

Well, five years from now, I will be forty-six and very likely will have less energy than I do currently, which means that it may not be as easy to study, work long hours, and do as many physical activities with my family as I am able to do now. I may or may not be living in Johannesburg, and if I am not, I may not have as much warm African weather as I enjoy currently, which may impact my energy levels and my motivation to carry out and complete tasks.

In five years, my son will be turning seventeen, and my daughter fifteen. They will be at very different life stages than they are currently. What will I miss about today, and what will I wish I had done differently?

For me, living it forward does not mean being preoccupied with the future and spending today planning tomorrow. Rather the focus is on taking some time to stand in the future and look back. What will today look like from the memory lens of tomorrow? Looking back, I consider what opportunities I could have taken hold of and used to create something of value—and more specifically, something of long-term or eternal value.

The problem with doing this is that many of today's opportunities really do appear to be merely inconveniences and nuisances that we really could live without. It's funny how time has a way of readjusting our perspectives. Perhaps it is the advantage of age and experience that helps us to see things differently years down the line. Whatever it is, what an advantage it would be if we had that foresight now, when we still have the opportunity to take hold of the moment and use it to create a more meaningful tomorrow.

So as hard as it is for most of us to admit, we've all had some missed opportunities that we really wish we could turn back the hands of time to seize.

Here's one of mine. In 2004, as a young graduate, I found myself working at a state-owned entity following a one-year internship program. The internship program had equipped me with a solid set of research skills, and I was excited to be working in the education sector. I had been placed in a relatively large office, which I shared with a consultant who was in her early fifties and very experienced in consulting, particularly in the field of education. We both reported to the same line manager, who also shared the office space.

I shared that office with Ansa for about a year, during which we formed a great cross-generational friendship. Our friendship continued thereafter, even though we both ended up with our own separate offices after a significant organizational restructure that left us both better off in terms of the nature and duration of our employment contracts.

She was a very present source of encouragement during my first pregnancy and made sure I was well-fed by providing me with all types of homemade jams, recipes, and other cooking tips. This was such a treasured time for me, and I hold those memories very dear right up to today.

While I had a very basic understanding of the work that Ansa did, my understanding remained purely superficial, and I always felt I was too busy coming to grips with the requirements of my own job to really spend time learning from her. One time she invited me to one of her committees, which was constituted of learning and development professionals from all corners of South Africa. Many of these members showed a great interest in me and commissioned me to conduct some desktop research for them, to assist them with some development work that they had to perform as a committee.

Ansa had briefed me well, so I was not totally unaware of the importance of the task; however, looking back, I realize that I really could have invested more time and effort in preparing for the task and learned a lot more from these passionate professionals.

Twelve years down the line, I am a consultant in the field of learning and development and have had to educate myself in all issues relating to education and training standards and the quality assurance processes relating to them. These are all lessons that I could have learned over the numerous coffees I had with Ansa during the time we shared office space and worked for the same organization. I strongly believe that had I invested time and interest in Ansa's work, I would have been better prepared when I began my consultancy and perhaps would have even formed stronger partnerships with some of those professional committee members who were keen to coach and direct me as a young graduate employee.

When we reflect back on missed opportunities, whatever the magnitude, we are often tempted to blame our lack of positive action on circumstances, obstacles, or people who were in one way or another part our lives.

Using my own example, I was in a new job, preoccupied with the demands of learning my own role, feeling somewhat demotivated at what appeared to be a relatively non-strategic first job, and later on was pregnant with my first child. These could all quite easily count as legitimate reasons for not stretching myself to grow my knowledge and skills, but I know these are merely excuses.

The "demands" of my first real job were really not that demanding, considering that my role was in fact on paper very "non-strategic." I had ample time between attending meetings and writing minutes to chat with Ansa and would have been welcome to attend any of her workshops had I requested this.

Furthermore, a "non-strategic" role on paper meant that I had carte blanche to make of the role whatever I felt would add value to the organization, but I chose not to do this. Instead I spent a considerable amount of time perfecting my non-strategic work, which is not a bad thing in itself but certainly not the highest priority looking back. I developed a system for writing minutes and making sure they were polished in record time and had perfected the art of developing meeting agendas and following up on key discussion points. I spent the rest of my work time reading up on possible research topics for future doctorates and reading up on what to expect during and after pregnancy. I was really bored and wished that someone could have given me some meaningful work to do.

So hindsight really is twenty-twenty vision. It's amazing now, twelve years down the line, how I regret my lack of initiative in learning other functional areas within the organization, when I could have directed my efforts toward improving the effectiveness of the committees that I served and focused my research hobby toward topics that would have enhanced the competitive advantage of the organization.

Fast-forward to 2013, when I was promoted to corporate services executive in a different organization, and the reality of the missed learning opportunities could not have been any more clear. Here I was sitting on the governing board and various other committees. By virtue of the position, I was a member of the organization's executive committee, and for the first time in my career, I was exposed to the interesting and somewhat complex world of analyzing business performance, scrutinizing the annual financial statements, and overseeing the annual report. In addition, a very significant part of my own personal dream was unraveling before my eyes. Soon after being promoted, I realized that my business wardrobe really would not suffice, and I needed to dress more professionally on a day-to-day basis. So out with the old "mommy clothes" that I had grown accustomed to wearing to work (no, I'm not kidding). I think I had about seven different outfits in total, which had allowed me to wear a different one to the office every day of the week. Of course, I could mix and match as well, which meant a few more options for the following week. But quite simply, my work clothes consisted of a few pairs of simple slacks, worn with mostly cotton semi-smart (and sometimes T-shirt) blouses with flat sandals. I casually accessorized that "mommy" wardrobe with simple studs and the occasional gold chain.

Suddenly, with the promotion came the demand for power-dressing. Not only was I opposed to the notion of power-dressing, but I also really did not believe it constituted value for money to any degree, and quite frankly, I thought of dressing up for work as a time-consuming inconvenience.

But during my first management meeting, I looked around at the other executives and suddenly felt very naked when I realized that every manager was donned in either a smart and stylish men's suit or a pencil skirt and pumps with stockings! It felt like something of an awakening, actually. I had always been the type of employee who was consumed with day-to-day business and the decisions that needed to be made on each particular day, and I paid no attention to those material things that had (in my opinion) no bearing on my personal performance at work or on the greater effectiveness of my team or department.

In fact, I had made it my mission to take a bold stand against any form of pressure to comply with the status quo, and woe betide any person who dared to comment on my dress sense (whether positive or negative).

You see, I had recently gone through my child-bearing years, and like any young mother coming back into the workplace, my life was suddenly far more complex than I had ever imagined possible. Gone were the childless days of waking up after 6:00 a.m. and actually having time to listen to the morning news while I leisurely got dressed up, did makeup, and styled my hair. Now the day began at 5:00 a.m. at the latest, with frantic and rather frustrating exercise (I did try very hard to fight off the pounds that I had gained) followed by a very quick shower. Thereafter, even paying any thought toward my clothes was a luxury that I was not going to entertain. So I would quickly throw on my simple and predictable clothes (I had actually perfected this to the extent that I knew which combination went with each day). Shoes were slipped on quickly, makeup was minimal, and earrings were often forgotten. I remember a few times walking into the ladies' bathroom after being at the office for an hour and discovering upon glancing in the mirror that I was wearing different earrings!

So you can imagine the whirlwind that I was living in, and hopefully, you can see how my job became something of an inconvenience in my life. You see, mothering has that effect. The home arena is never the inconvenience. It is everything else that needs to slow down and make way for the new you. That is how I felt. I was a very fulfilled mother, although like any other mother, I had hopes of spending even more time with my family than I was doing at the time.

So my promotion is not quite an example of a missed opportunity, but I don't claim that I embraced it with both hands when it came along either. I was in a beautiful arrangement of working half days in order to spend time with the children but also bring an income into the home and build my career, albeit slower than before. This was quite a perfect position for our family. Yes, we had reduced our household income when my hours were reduced, but we were very thankful that we were still able to meet our financial obligations, and our household was in a healthier state with my increased home presence.

There's no such thing as a "half-day job" of course, particularly if you hold any form of management position. So yes, I could walk out of the office at lunchtime and enter the exciting world of school runs, enjoy warm hugs as I collected kids, and participate in the fun activities of the afternoon, including homework. But my laptop and cell phone remained close by to ensure that I did not miss out on an office crisis or a critical instruction from my boss.

I learned to live with this. After all, there are sacrifices involved with most things that are worth having. I had this role perfected and often put in some time during weekends to catch up on work or just make sure that I didn't fall behind. In fact, I was the type of employee who thrived on being ahead. You see, preparation is definitely one of my strengths, and ever since my teenage years, when I grew accustomed to waking up to study in the middle of the night, I have been sold on the idea of preparing in advance for almost everything.

Then I had my superwoman season when I dropped kids off in the morning, left the office at midday to drive to the school in time to collect them from class, rushed to drop them off at home, and then sped back to the office by 2:00 p.m. and stayed slightly later to make up for my long lunch. Unsurprisingly, this was a great source of exhaustion (and backache), but I stuck it out for about six months because it gave me the sweet reward of seeing those happy smiles as my children ran into my arms after school broke up.

I guess life's really not easy for a mom.

ALL EYES DOWNCAST

By virtue of its very nature, executive leadership is challenging on a day-to-day basis. It is not so much the technical aspects of the job as it is the issues with leading people. The importance of communicating frequently and efficiently as well as keeping staff motivated cannot be overestimated.

However, despite the day-to-day challenges, it is possible to face and overcome the difficult situations, even though some take longer than others to resolve. For all my brilliance in preparation, I found it virtually impossible to be completely prepared for the situations that arose on a daily or weekly basis. Just when I thought I had my work mapped out and could focus some time on developing new aspects of the organization, along came an unforeseen situation that would often threaten the reputation or performance of the organization or the credibility of the management team. Eventually, I surrendered the hope of ever being prepared for crises and learned to take each day as it came and to make use of the incredible people resources that surrounded me.

As experience grew, so did the challenges. Just when you think you've dealt with every possible scenario, a curveball is just around the corner.

It was 2014. I had settled well into my role and felt I was finally coping and performing above average. I discovered an error in one of our stakeholder payment calculations and was determined to correct the error to ensure full compliance. After bringing the issue to the attention of my boss, I felt I had his full backing and threw myself wholeheartedly into analyzing the extent of the error and putting a process in place to correct it.

I had finally completed my analysis and was very pleased with my efforts. It was a Tuesday morning, and as usual the management meeting would begin at 9:30 a.m. After my boss had completed his report and various related discussions, I let the other managers proceed with their reports, and finally toward the end of the meeting, I had an opportunity to present my own report.

After I gave an eloquent explanation of the error and my plan for correction, my boss reflected audibly on what appeared to be the political implications of my corrective plan. He articulated his concern regarding the reaction of these critical stakeholders and anticipated that the corrective measures would not be well-received. Adamant about obtaining written approval (a trait I had quickly acquired once on the executive team), I decided to remain silent in order to give him an opportunity to reflect before coming to an agreement that we needed to urgently implement my plan. Much to my despair, this did not happen. What followed next was a series of sympathizing comments from my colleagues, who agreed with my boss's concerns over the anticipated reaction of stakeholders. Some of them joked about the potential reactions, and the humor served to temporarily decrease the tension in the room.

It was at that point when my eyes opened to the realization of what was going on in this boardroom. My boss was unwilling to implement corrective measures because he feared a negative response from these critical members. He could not quite bring himself to articulate this, and he most certainly did not want it minuted. Eventually, with quick thinking and quick calculating, he presented a counterproposal and announced that this would be a far better solution in terms of the response that it was likely to receive; it would deliver a much softer blow to the stakeholders. The only problem with his counterproposal was that it would result in board members earning more than the permissible amounts, thereby resulting in the organization being in breach of policy.

The breathing exercises that I had learned during my prenatal classes finally came in handy. (I had prescheduled cesarean sections when I delivered both my children, so I had never had the opportunity to use them!) I found myself taking a few deep, deliberate breaths and exhaling purposefully in a quest to maintain inner and outer peace.

My husband will tell you that I do not back down easily. This trait is exceptionally aggravated in situations where I have data and analysis on my side.

So there we went again. This time I pointed out that my boss's proposal was not feasible because it would still not present an accurate and compliant status. I repeated my correction plan, this time emphasizing the long-term benefits of achieving accuracy and compliance and noting that the short-term inconvenience to the stakeholders would contribute toward a more open and honest relationship with them in the long run. (I tried really hard to avoid blatantly labeling my boss's proposal as dishonest). He disagreed. You see, he was equally stubborn, and now he was outrightly disagreeing with my proposal.

I felt myself shaking on the inside. I soon forgot about the prenatal breathing techniques and let out a sigh. I had no option but to point out to him that any other proposal would be dishonest and that we would run the risk of having to defend it in court if it came to that.

Yet he still refused. He had come to a compromised position that he felt would bring about a level of correction and retain the relationship that he enjoyed with these stakeholders.

I felt more desperate than ever before. I did all that I knew how at that stage. I highlighted the benefits of my proposal and emphasized the importance of doing the right thing. As I paused, I realized the gravity of the moment. This was a pivotal moment for me. If I let this one go, I would never be able to stand up for anything else that was ethical in this organization again.

I had gone as far as I could with the data. It was time to engage the politics and the ethics. I remembered that there were three other executives who could potentially assist me with obtaining approval of my plan. In the heat of the tense information exchanges between my boss and myself, I had forgotten they were present. The room had grown eerily silent as the "tennis match" between my boss and myself had advanced.

This time I began my appeal by turning toward each and every one of them. I appealed to their sense of morality and their commitment to compliance. I looked at one, then the other, and then the next. The reaction I got was the same each time. As soon as I began my appeal and caught their eyes, all eyes were downcast.

I felt an overwhelming sense of disappointment to say the least. I had felt their eyes on me as I had argued my point to my boss. They were okay to watch this interesting exchange like a movie. I guess it was somewhat entertaining from the outside. However, none were willing to stand with me. Not one. It shook me to the core.

There was silence in the boardroom. I sighed and took one more look around the room. My boss was checking his emails on his phone, my colleagues were still staring at the wood patterns of the boardroom table, and only one pair of eyes met mine. It was the committee secretary. She looked at me with what appeared to be intrigue and smiled before joining the wood analyzers in the room.

I sat back in my chair. What I felt was exhaustion, a headache, and despair. What a moment. This was the day I realized that I did not know my colleagues as well as I had thought I did.

One of them finally broke the tension with a joke, and we

were promptly reminded that time was running out, and we needed to close the meeting within the next few minutes. My boss announced the resolution of my agenda item by detailing his counterproposal for the purpose of minuting. Because I had already indicated that I was unwilling to implement the incomplete plan, he volunteered to personally sign approvals for the payments himself. Meeting closed.

I don't think the rest of that day was in the least bit productive. You see, you can work with a team of people and believe that you are equally committed to the organization and even that you share the same moral compass, but this is not always true. I recently learned of a theory named the over-consensus theory, which suggests that most people overestimate the extent to which other people agree with their values, perceptions, or opinions. The theory is appropriately explained in the context of leadership as a forewarning for leaders. How I wish I had had this insight then.

Until you get to a critical point of decision such as this, you really don't know what relationship your colleagues have with the organization, what their true interests are, or what their moral standards are.

Bonus season was around the corner, and it became an understood fact that I would get the least percentage bonus after my unforgettable management meeting. I made peace with that.

I made peace with a number of thoughts after that meeting, and quite frankly, the bonus was the least of my concerns. My real concerns lay in the type of future that I had in the organization, considering my observations of my colleagues in that meeting.

Would I ever really be able to bring about the type of change that I hoped to see in the organization? My mission was to change the entity, and I had planned to do it through ethics and people development. How would this work with this kind of team?

Driving home, I was on autopilot. I replayed the meeting over and over in my mind and looked for fault in my approach. Had I been too strong today? Was I disrespectful? Was I unreasonable? I even revisited the counterproposal —did it make sense? Perhaps I had not fully understood it and had dismissed it without due consideration.

No. This was much more than just going into a meeting and having your proposal turned down. This was a loss to the organization—a great one that would have future implications. It would create a precedent for when the rules were not followed, and it would be easier to repeat this response and take other shortcuts in the future.

My mind zoomed out from the organization, and I reflected upon government. *This is how it begins,* I thought. *This is just a microcosm of government. It begins in a small management meeting where the truth loses the vote.*

But it should be so simple, I thought. *We all knew what the right thing was. What kept my colleagues from giving me their support?* I reflected on each of them and realized that they were all very competent managers who seemed to work long and hard for the good of the organization. What was so wrong with disagreeing with the boss for the greater good?

I would never have the answers. All I knew at the time was that my colleagues for some reason had not been willing to voice their opinions on the important matter. After all, it did not fall directly within their business areas, and they had not felt any pressure to take a verbal vote. Their silence was enough, though, and their downcast eyes would never be erased from my memory.

Do we all really have a price? I wondered. I begged to disagree.

POWER, POLITICS, AND MUCH ADO ABOUT A SANDWICH

I 've always prided myself on my lack of conformity to politics and political tactics. I remember studying my honors degree in human resources development and having to learn a section on power and politics. I was simply unimpressed at the tactics that leaders use to get others to follow them and vowed that I would never confirm to any of these. You see, I had it all figured out. I would stick to the knitting, as they say, and my technical delivery would be so sharp that there would be no need for politics.

Boy, was I wrong! Going back to my previous example, politics was just another form of background noise. No matter how significant the strength of the desired signal, the noise causes so much interference that the results simply do not make sense.

I learned this when I first began to work with the board.

My boss swung into my office one morning to announce that the board's chairperson had arrived, and she was in her office, which was a few steps from mine. He wanted to introduce me to her. *Oh boy*, I thought, because I really was no good at niceties and casual chitchat. I felt nervous because I had heard that she was a tough woman with very strong political connections and affiliations.

She was hunched over her desk when I walked in with my boss. I suddenly felt very aware of myself and wondered if the suit I was wearing that day was up to standard. My boss greeted her with great enthusiasm and received a very dry and formal response. That made me even more uneasy. I didn't want to sound too enthusiastic, but I certainly did not want to come across as unfriendly or disinterested.

Once official introductions had been made, she looked me up and down, and I held my breath. I was prepared with all my management experience and had my knowledge of corporate governance at my fingertips. But what came out of her mouth at that point was completely surprising and caught me unawares. "Did you say your surname was Ndou? Do any of your relatives work for the ruling party?"

Wow, my brain had never worked so hard. It was such a simple question, but I knew my answer would be of some significance to this important person. With my heart beating even faster this time, I reeled off the names of all my brothers-in-law who currently worked for government. She asked me whether any of them were based in Limpopo, and after I explained that my father-in-law had been a freedom activist who had been buried by both the ruling party and the church, I knew that I had passed the test. A thin smile spread across her stern face, and our introductory meeting was over as soon as she announced, "Welcome to the executive team!"

A few months into my executive career, I had perfected the art of VFL. "Visible and felt leadership" had been an important management behavior for my previous employer, and I was adamant to keep it alive and well wherever I went. I encouraged my direct reports to follow suit. So I practiced what I preached. I took walks down to the first floor to oversee the operations, in particular the preparation of critical governance documents, and to maintain my management presence within the division and the organization. Typically, I would arrive on the floor to find a busy and loud open-plan office with much laughter and chatter as staff collected printed documents, punched holes in them, perforated plastic covers, and bound documents into beautifully neat board packs.

On one of my VFL visits one Wednesday morning, I was rather vexed when I arrived in the open-plan office to find the governance administrator carrying a baby on her back! After inquiring, I was promptly informed (by more than one person, simultaneously) that the baby belonged to one of the board members and that she had gotten into the habit of bringing her baby to meetings when she was unable to secure a babysitter.

Of course, I thought the situation was ridiculous, and I pointed out all of the hazards of having a baby in our very busy administrative office space. But my words were all in vain, and I knew it. It appeared that my boss knew of the arrangement and had expressed his displeasure, but in order to keep political noise at a minimum, he had turned a blind eye.

As I turned around to exit the room, I never would have guessed the repercussions of my next actions. Walking past the governance administrator (with the baby on her back), I reached out as naturally as any other mother would and removed a piece of fluff from the baby's hair as I exited the office.

The next morning, I was greeted by the CEO's personal assistant, who seemed to be waiting for my arrival. Judging by the number of people gathered around her, I was certain something was very wrong, and she did not leave me in suspense for too long. As swiftly as she could reel the words off her tongue, she told me of the dramatic events that had unfolded the previous afternoon when the baby's mother had come out of her meeting to collect her bundle of joy. Apparently, she had inquired after the strand of hair that she had been nurturing in order to add it to her son's baby book. After hearing of my "fluff" removal action, she had become enraged and left the building extremely upset.

I was dumbstruck. How on earth did I manage to get myself

into these situations? All I really wanted was a challenging management position in which I could grow my skills and confidence and make a significant difference to the organization. Now I was implicated in personal affairs involving babies and hair strand collections! Really?

For all my shock and disbelief, there was no way of getting around it. By the time I got to the next management meeting, my boss was in stitches, and he shared the comical events with my colleagues, who were equally amused. I was promptly advised to write a formal apology to the board member, profusely expressing regret at the unfortunate incident regarding her baby's hair, and to wait patiently for pardon.

It was at that moment that my rational mind began to wage war. Wait a minute—a board member brings a baby to a meeting and asks for a personal babysitting favor from a staff member, which is against the policies of the organization, and a blind eye is turned. Then I attempt to remove fluff from the baby's hair, and I need to produce a written apology? What kind of world were we living in?

The silent agreement over my need to apologize was accepted by the senior management team, and as ludicrous as I thought it was, I wrote the apology and sent it off. In addition, I offered a face-to-face apology at the next board meeting, and my sins were forgiven. Peace was restored between the management team and the board. I guess politics doesn't have to make sense.

So that was my first encounter with that level of politics, but it was by no means the last. A few years thereafter, I was faced with what could have been an even more bizarre phenomenon involving a board member and a sandwich.

I don't think anyone in that executive wing will ever forget it. It started off like any ordinary day. A special meeting of the Human Resources and Remuneration Committee was scheduled to begin at 2:00 p.m., and a board member had confirmed her attendance. As was the case whenever she was expected in the office, staff members were rushing to and fro, preparing for her visit. A few months prior, she had expressed her displeasure at the quality of cutlery that she had been presented with. Thereafter, the CEO's personal assistant had promptly paid a visit to Adam's (a reputable homeware store) to purchase the best-quality cutlery they had.

Fortunately, today there was no need for cutlery and crockery. The 2:00 p.m. meeting required only tea and coffee for the committee members. My own assistant had taken it upon herself to prepare the board member's office according to her requirements. Her newly delivered leather furniture had been thoroughly cleaned and polished, and there was an air of peace and tranquility in the executive wing.

By two o'clock I had joined my two management staff and another executive who were sitting in the committee room, awaiting the arrival of other committee members. The board member walked into the room, seemingly flustered and distracted. As was the norm, she was juggling answering phone calls and responding to emails via her mobile. My personal assistant was behind her, carrying her workbag, and the board member muttered that she was starving and requested a chicken and mayo sandwich.

My ears twitched, and as I turned to look at my assistant, I could tell we were both thinking the same thing. I quickly followed her out of the room and instructed her to call the local sandwich franchise. Our own canteen was not going to cut it, and I was not willing to take the risk of her lunch going wrong before such an important meeting.

After we had clarified the exact requirements of this chicken and mayo sandwich (never take anything for granted), the order was placed, and a corporate sigh of relief was breathed—all too soon.

I caught the tail end of what followed a while later—something that sounded like an exasperated scream and a loud bang. What could be taking place in the boardroom? I walked in and caught the incredulous glares of my staff and the other executive. The board member marched past me and out of the room. "How difficult can it be to get a sandwich around here?"

I must confess, it was only then that I remembered the ordered chicken and mayo sandwich. Half an hour later, the delivery man had not arrived, and the board member had descended like a ton of bricks on anyone who was within earshot.

She had just gotten off a flight from Cape Town, and quite clearly, she had missed lunch, and now she was absolutely starved, and her sandwich was not materializing nearly as quickly as she willed it to.

Wow! There was a deathly silence in that room. Every manager was still standing in exactly the spot that I had found them in, with the same look of absolute disbelief. Was all of this happening because of a sandwich? Or rather the lack thereof?

It was then that one of my staff members broke the silence as she whispered 'never leave home without a fruit in your bag'. My dad had taught me that growing up, but I honestly had never thought that forgetting it could result in a tantrum of these proportions.

So there we had it—a lesson learned right before our eyes. Ensuring you are well-fed is a critical factor in personal leadership. After all, when you have up to four meetings nearly back-to-back in one day, it is possible that you may end up forfeiting breakfast and lunch, and by two o'clock, you will be not only desperately famished but also downright furious at anyone standing inconsiderately between you and your chicken and mayo sandwich.

THE FIVE STAGES
OF GRIEF

Stage 1: Are You Kidding Me?

Okay, so a lot had happened in my working life, but here I was in 2017. One might have describe me as a "stay-at-home mom," but I still didn't know what that actually meant.

"Stay-at-home" really just sounded like everyone leaves the house in the morning, and you're the one who stays behind. But that was nothing like what my life was really felt like at that point in time. I mean, if I just "stayed at home," there would need to be someone to get the children organized and seated in the car on time and someone to drive them to school. Also, "staying at home" seemed to involve no reference to actual work, which was inevitable for a stay-at-home mom really.

I would typically get back home from the school run, and feel I was under pressure to be productive. I mean, I had spent the past fourteen years (after graduating with my first master's degree) waking up at the crack of dawn to hit the traffic, listen passively to the radio while moving in slow inches toward my office, and then face the pressure and politics of an organization for another eight hours. It seemed that was what we all became accustomed to. We adapted to the rat race and couldn't imagine what life would be like if we opted out. Of course, I had fantasized about being a woman of leisure and had imagined spending copious amounts of time at champagne breakfasts and tea parties, but in reality, the financial pressures accompanying being at home did not allow for these activities to become the norm.

So there I was … at home.

I was not a housewife, because that would imply that my sole responsibility was to manage the household and tend to the needs of my husband and nothing else. But that was not true for me. After opting out of formal employment, I had never felt more pressure to generate an income as I did then.

I had registered the business—that was the easy part. I had always wanted to have my own business, and I had long imagined what it would look and feel like. I saw myself in my mind's eye, standing before many corporate clients, and the very thought of it was exciting and somewhat impressive even to myself.

However, since then, the day-to-day reality had been nothing like I had imagined! Now that the business was registered, the website was up and running, business cards were printed, and I was 100 percent available to work, the phone was not ringing, and there were no emails. Okay, there were emails from Facebook, healthy living websites, wannabe writers' forums, and other people looking for customers and clients for all forms of products and services.

As a result of the difficult season, I had to say goodbye to my working-mom luxuries, which were but a distant memory. Gone were the stopovers at Woolworths on the way home to spoil the children; far away were my occasional stopovers at the mall to spoil myself with new work clothing or shoes; and almost forgotten were family Sunday lunches out at Mugg & Bean, where we would sit with the children and dine for a couple of hours on a lazy afternoon.

Wow, had I really had all of that? It was almost hard to imagine, looking back from where I was. I guess it pays to have a sense of humor about these things. I mean, I never would have imagined that I would be in a position where I would have to open my purse in Pick 'n' Pay to literally count the coins I had before reaching out for a carton of milk or a loaf of bread. Oh, those memories of picking and choosing the healthiest loaf of bread and the luxury of being able to embark on a protein diet. At that moment, it didn't matter whether the bread was low GI or whether it was extra wheat with honey and oat (which used to be a favorite of mine). I just needed to make ends meet. I figured, if I got the R7.99 loaf (which is just a plain white loaf, straight out of the oven, completely refined, but hey, it's bread!), I would have enough coins left over to buy my son the disposable juice bottle he needed for his class trip the next day. As long as it worked, no one was particularly phased by the fact that we didn't get the healthiest bread on offer.

The clothing situation was another no-go. Fortunately, because I had been considerably privileged in my previous working life, I had a lot of good-quality clothes. Thanks to a great executive salary package and the fact that I was a fully grown adult and had managed to maintain my size over the past couple of years, everything still fitted. Unfortunately, that was not the case for the children. Gone were the days of taking the children out for biannual clothes shopping, where we would spend a couple of thousand rand on clothing for each child, from good-quality clothing stores, to make sure they were well prepared for winter or summer, or whichever season we happened to be embarking upon. Unfortunately, all that was left of that was cupboards filled with beautiful-quality coats, boots, cargos, and sweaters, which don't fit anyone in the family but were at least a blessing to younger cousins in various parts of the country and the world.

Not to mention the ache of looking at my son in his only pair of very faded jeans and the only jacket that still fitted, which happened to also be his favorite, whose blue and gray designs could just barely be made out anymore. Or my daughter's daily outfit choices which were made up of tights (always tights) with a skirt that she had clearly outgrown and a very tight vest, the only one that still fitted, with the old faithful purple coat that was more than three years old.

So quite frankly, this was the sort of situation that you may have heard that someone else was going through and you felt really bad for the them and hoped that things would turn around quickly, before thankfully returning to your own life, albeit imperfect. It was that awkward season that your friend goes through, and you are quite faithful about praying for her daily and even helping her out with some groceries here and there, but really can't imagine dwelling on for too long because it was downright depressing and unpleasant.

Off course when it's happening to you it is incomprehensible, to put it lightly. I struggled to come to terms with the fact that I was going through all of this after two master's degrees and executive-level professional experience in my previous working life.

On good days I told myself that I would surely bounce back from this tremendous mess. All I needed to do was make sure that word didn't get round too much about my financial crisis. If I could just cover the gaps and attend to all the essentials, I wouldn't need to explain myself to anyone. I had gone through the entire "get out of debt and stay out" lesson in the wellness program at work, and I was the living example of being debt-free. So apart from necessary debt like the mortgage, I really had no debt. I was living in a cash society, and I loved it. All I needed now was a bit more cash and much more cash-flow.

On harder days I instructed myself to simply work harder at the business and make it work. I had all the education I needed and all the work experience, and now I just need to be a bit more positive and confident and go out there and make a success of the company and of myself. It couldn't be that hard … could it?

On really tough days, I tried really hard to avoid depressing conversations with my husband. Some days I felt like he thought he was the only financially literate individual in our household. I also wasn't always sure what to make of his depressing conversations (or monologues) on how severe our financial situation was (I already spent hours meditating on this most days) and the fact that we would be in serious trouble if things didn't turn around soon. I was grateful that he acknowledged my efforts toward starting and growing the business, but I really couldn't handle discussing it much. The fact is I knew that things were really serious and that we might even lose some of our investments if we didn't increase our income, but I didn't know how to turn that morbid conversation into business revenue. If I did, we'd have been pretty rich by then.

I guess it had been hard to come to terms with the seriousness of the situation because every time I thought we had hit rock bottom, my husband had pulled some money out of a hat, and we would be okay again. That certainly happened a few times, and each time I was left breathing a sigh of relief and marveling at this hero I married who just seemed to step in at the right time to save the day!

But lately, it had been getting hard for him too; I had noticed that. I also noticed him spending hours on our family budget, changing figures and making projections and trying to squeeze money out of a stone almost. I must admit, it seemed to put me in a state of panic, but it had the most positive impact on my prayer life; it almost always led me to deeper and richer prayer times as I had to trust sincerely for our daily bread.

I guess I refused to lose hope. I knew this season had to end sometime and that it would turn around eventually. I held on to every word of scripture and every encouragement sent to me by friends and family. I also managed to get the children to start praying for the business, and I believe they began to see the link between trusting for the business to grow and the provision of their many needs.

During that difficult season, my husband announced for the first time that his secret emergency fund had run out and that we were not likely to make month-end commitments. I felt really confused—not afraid, just confused. It felt a little like being in a bubble; as if you're not really in your own life, and you're almost just watching it all unfold. There was no way this could be real because we had never been here before. There had always been someplace to draw from; even when we'd run out of provisions in the house, there had always been a little pocket to resort to and a glimmer of hope.

I guess age had taught me not to waste time worrying about things I could not change. I focused my thoughts and feelings on praying for the situation. There was no way that we could actually go through a month-end of unpaid bills. That had never happened, and I refused to believe it was our portion. There is freedom in faith. I didn't feel overwhelmed, and I certainly did not feel like I needed to be calling around borrowing money. I aligned all my efforts towards working on the business—getting myself and the business out there, making contacts, joining networks. I was confident it would all pay off. And I was so ready for the miracle that was coming. I was more expectant than I had ever been before. There was no way that month-end would come around and roll past with unpaid bills. I made every single confession that a person could make with their mouth to command a turnaround. I exhaled, knowing that salvation was on its way. Yes, I was nervous, but I was expecting a miracle, and I knew it would surely come to pass just in time.

Stage 2: Can Anyone Hear Me?

Ping! Ping! Ping! That was the sound from my iPhone when I switched it on that morning. It was the first of the month, and the bank had obviously developed an obsession with me overnight.

Repeated messages informed me that transactions had been declined due to insufficient funds in my checking account. And the bank just had to send an alert for each one of the six or seven debits that had not been successful! One would think they would have gotten the message after the second or third transaction. There is no money in that account—get the message already! I haven't been working for a while, and you should have picked that up after the first few months without the regular deposit on the twenty-fifth.

I was frustrated and desperate. Why was all of this happening to me when I was praying and trusting for my situation to turn around? Speaking to my husband was useless, I felt. Despite my constant nagging and pleas that he deposit money into my account, he did nothing. Finally, I got it. There was no money left, and his endless depressing murmurs about our finances had been justified. There was nothing left. He had done everything he could, and now there was nothing left. This had to be someone's fault. Someone ought to take the blame or at least take responsibility for the situation we were in. It was irresponsible for two adults to be in this situation. I felt angry and entitled. It certainly was not my fault. I had done everything that my logical mind knew to do, and it had yielded no results. And after all, I was a woman—no, sorry, I was a wife. And I had a husband and my faith. So one of the two would surely come through to change this situation and soon.

That was that. I was stark raving mad, and I had made myself clear, albeit in my heart and mind. I was going to be steady and steadfast about being upset. So I spent the next few days in hostile anticipation. I had prayed and felt like I understood the responsibility and accountability order, and I was sticking to my guns. I operated in my cold and detached fury for days. I woke up, exercised, prepared the children for school, took them to school, came back home, and ate my breakfast in cold fury. I read the Bible and prayed (mostly in between angry tears). How was all of this happening to me? What had I done wrong? It really couldn't be so hard to provide the money we needed. We had prayed for and seen so many miracles for so many people before. Why couldn't we get the breakthrough we were seeking? I had reached the height of frustration and desperately needed someone to blame. And before long, I had found that "someone."

As if our financial situation was not severe enough on its own, an unexpected problem was brewing simultaneously, and the worse our financial pressures grew, the more desperate the problem became. My husband and I had invested some money with a company owned by an acquaintance. As a result of a miscalculated risk, the company owner had invested the funds in a project that turned out to be hugely problematic, and our interest payments had been withheld for many months. Although this situation was aggravating our financial pressures, it was by no means the cause of our problem, but that didn't matter to me at the time. I desperately needed someone to blame, and I had found that party. If only we could receive these payments, we would be able to pay all of our monthly obligations for a few months and be out of the red. I felt angry about this. How could all of this be happening to us all at once? What were we expected to do? We had a number of rental properties as well as our own home mortgage to worry about, not to mention school fees and other living expenses.

I was angry, and I needed an outlet. I decided to share my grief with my family on our girls' WhatsApp group. I described the gravity of our situation, asked for prayer, vented, cried, complained, asked for advice, accepted advice, gave daily updates, received prayer, and cried some more. This situation was unfair; I was convinced of it. I didn't believe there was anything for us to learn from it because we had been quite responsible with our finances for years and were not deserving of this misfortune.

As it happened, our misfortune continued. Month-end had come and gone, and bills had gone unpaid. I vowed that I would not ignore phone calls since I had done nothing wrong and had nothing to hide. I was not quite prepared for the hate mail I received from my cell phone provider, though. My service would be switched off in twenty-four hours if I didn't pay the due amount immediately. Really? That had never happened to me before. It's really funny how quickly they forget your perfect payment record. At the first sign of trouble, they threaten to cut you off.

And they aren't the only ones, you know. Once it begins, the chain reaction is activated, and you're no longer sure whether you're actually alive or watching a really embarrassing movie of yourself. Take the gym for instance. They love you when you're paying them on time, and they send you a lot of useless happy mail. But cross them once with a bounced debit, and the love is gone. So true to my religious Tuesday and Thursday morning routine, I left the children at school and headed off to the gym for my much-loved and much-deserved Pilates class. I was greeted enthusiastically by one of the gym staff as she activated my card to give me entry to the gym. There was a beep and then a manual intervention that gave me access. I was instantly suspicious that my bounced debit had been registered and my days of organized stretching and physical fitness were numbered. But I pressed on like the confident professional I was.

On my next visit to the gym, I was greeted by a not-so-friendly staff member who asked me whether I was aware of the underpayment on my gym account. Taken aback by the confrontation, I mumbled something about checking with my husband, and she obliged as I promised to get the problem addressed soon.

I wasn't so lucky on my third visit. This time a very unfriendly and unfamiliar staff member told me that she could not give me access to the gym because there was an outstanding balance on my account. Any innocent customer would have swiped their bank card there and then, rendering that unpleasant situation history in the blink of an eye. That, of course, was way too simple to be applicable to me. With no funds in my account, there was nothing I could do to make the unpleasant situation go away, so I had no recourse except to stress to the receptionist that I was late for my Pilates class and that I would attend to the underpayment when I got home. *What in the world have I become?* I wondered.

As soon as I got home, I crawled into bed and covered my head. This really could not be my life. Never in a thousand years could I have imagined that I would be turned away from the gym for non-payment! I admitted it. I had hit rock bottom, and there was only one way from here: up. *Help me!* I thought.

I certainly was not prepared for what my husband had gone through that very day. When he arrived home a full one and half hours before his usual arrival time, there was much merriment in the house, and the kids rushed to hug him and inquire about his day. This time, even he couldn't keep our troubles from the children. Our son asked him how his day had been, and he promptly replied, "Terrible." Sure, he immediately changed his response to "Just kidding—it was fine, my boy," but I knew something wasn't right.

I followed him into our room, where he had kicked off his shoes and was strewn on the bed, head down and eyes closed. He didn't wait for my question. "The municipality has switched us off." He had received the call from our holiday rental apartment that afternoon. The municipality had arrived on site and were switching us off that very moment.

Wow. It's amazing how these experiences deliver you instantaneously from the opinions of people and focus you on what really matters. For exactly one second, I imagined the amount of gossip that situation had stirred up at the reception desk of the holiday complex, but I immediately concluded that didn't matter. They could talk as much as they wanted; I really didn't care. But I didn't want to lose that property. We had bought it during a very difficult time, and a large amount of income had already gone into it.

I stood and watched my husband. He was lying motionless on that bed, attenuated. *Okay, he's given up,* I thought. I was not going to stand there and watch him give up. I was swinging between pity and anger the entire time. The poor man had, for the very first time ever in our marriage, come home early because he had had a bad day. That was not his style. It was more my style, I must admit. He was always the guy who took whatever came on the chin and then vented briefly in the evening before getting on with it again the next day. He was home early, lying defeated on the bed and appearing to have given up. I prayed silently and desperately. *Help!*

Stage 3: Fast and Beg

I wasn't going to give up. My husband began the property-selling dialogue soon after his bad day. He explained that he might be able to get a good price on the seaside apartment if he put it up for sale now. I felt light-headed listening to him. Had he finally lost the plot? That apartment was my current retirement plan, and my mind refused to even try to conceptualize this possibility. I felt guilty even trying to convince him to leave the properties alone. He was receiving telephone calls from the bank daily, which was clearly stressing him out.

As if our situation wasn't bad enough, two of our tenants in other rental properties had begun to default on their rent, and this was placing us in an even more difficult position. I felt tired when Steve got home at the end of each day. What else would he have to tell me today? Had our situation gotten any worse? Had he made any unilateral decisions and put up one of the properties for sale? I was arriving at the dinner table a few minutes later each time. I felt like my heavy sighs were amplified around our small table of four. In addition, I felt like I was the only one feeling that way. My husband had a way of picking himself up around the children and conducting a "normal" conversation with them, inquiring about their days at school and the activities of the afternoon. The children were, as usual, cheerful and full of lively stories from the happenings at school. It seemed I was the only gloomy member.

Before long, I had it all figured out. We must have done something wrong to deserve this. I wasn't sure what it was, but I was certainly going to get us out of this situation. All I needed to do was prove that I was sorry and that I could be trusted with much. What better way than to fast and pray? I had actually gotten the sense that I should dedicate some time to prayer.

So I embarked on a three-day fast and prayer session. Well prepared with liters of juice and loads of tea and coffee, I began the fast. It was a rewarding time for me, and I certainly felt that many issues were settled in my heart during that time. For the first time in a really long time, I was able to let go of my life and surrender all of my anxieties. It really wasn't for me to worry about my bills and what we would eat or drink. I felt that I had fully submitted all my concerns and that I could rest and trust for a miracle.

I really believe that as strange as it was, the act of fasting gave me a sense of endeavor regarding our seemingly hopeless situation. Instead of sitting around eating and drinking, I fasted. I prayed during mealtimes and felt as though I was committedly doing something about our situation.

At the same time, I believe that a really essential transformation for me was my attitude toward all of the obligations that we had. Apart from feeling freed from anxiety around our bills and financial situation, I felt an overwhelming sense of relief as I realized that I didn't have to do so many of those discretionary and costly activities that we had all gotten used to. There was the children's participation in the National Eisteddfod Association for drama, for example. The children had become used to taking part in this exciting program and had done so over the past four years. So understandably, when we announced to them that it was not financially possible for us to participate this year, we were met with a level of sorrow around the decision. And it broke our hearts, like it would any parents', to think that we were unable to afford this for them. Fortunately, our son is an ever-upbeat kind of guy who quickly accepted the situation and was able to embrace the advantages of having his Saturdays free for the next three months; there were many things that a boy could plan to do with his Saturday afternoons. Personally, I looked for the opportunity in this dilemma and very quickly found hope in the fact that this would free up our children to enjoy some time at home and give our son some time to focus on his swimming once winter was gone. Of course, this was contingent upon us being able to afford swimming lessons when the time came, but that was a concern for another season.

Our daughter, on the other hand, lives for performing. She was distraught at the very thought of not participating in drama eisteddfods this year. Even though I explained over and over again that she would still take part in singing eisteddfod and would pick up on drama in the coming year, she was inconsolable. We were thankful for her easygoing brother, who not only pointed out the advantages of having some free weekends but also helped her appreciate the importance of making sacrifices during our financial crisis.

Where had these children come from? My emotions were a bittersweet mixture of sincere pride at having such levelheaded and disciplined children and sorrow over not being able to please my children. I knew it was for a season, though, and that gave me courage personally.

All I had to do now was focus myself on fasting and prayer, and I was sure I would be rewarded for my faithfulness. I even accepted the issue of timing, knowing that there was no better season than the appointed season, and I was willing to wait (within reason, of course!).

In all honesty, I was able to resign to our situation because I was sure it was going to turn around quickly. I made peace with the fact that we couldn't just choose what we wanted to have for supper like we had grown accustomed to. Now I had to think about what was actually in the cupboard and live with having repeat options for days and weeks on end. In these moments, it feels a little like you're a tire, and you're lying in the sun with almost all of the air let out from you. I got used to walking past shops without paying any mind to what was in the window. This was very different from where I had been when I first left my job. Then I used to stare longingly at shop windows and wish for the days when money was overflowing, when I could walk in and buy whatever I pleased. Of course, time had always been the issue then. I always seemed to be working and felt guilty for not spending every waking hour with the children when I had the chance. Now I had the gift of time, which was ever so precious, I'd be the first to admit. But why did the two need to be mutually exclusive? Okay, I do actually have logic and common sense, so I don't need anyone to explain that to me, but how come celebrities and the royal family get to have it all? It is so unfair!

So here I was, walking in the mall only on the rare occasion when it was absolutely necessary. And even then, I couldn't afford to look at and long after stuff. I almost always had exactly the amount that I needed to buy what I was there for, and then I made my way quickly to the car.

The car—I had never been so aware that it runs on fuel as I was now. And even worse, that fuel could be so costly! I mean, really, is there nothing free in this world? I mean apart from the fruits of the Spirit.

So that was my life at the moment, getting on with it and looking forward to a quick turnaround. The longer the tire sits in the scorching sun, the hotter and flatter it gets. Quite honestly, I was at a point where I simply did not react to anything anymore.

So the crying pity parties continued: arrive home, park the

car, and sit in the car for at least another half hour, listening to worship music and crying. Why couldn't we be miraculously rescued? I felt that I was suffering terribly, even though my husband had different views on the matter.

As I sat in the car crying, I reflected on all of the missed opportunities. So many friends had gone through difficult times and had asked for prayer, and that was all I had given them. How I wished I could go back in time and give them money or groceries or gift vouchers. Was this what they had been through? I struggled to deal with my lack of compassion. How could I have let my heart grow so cold and detached? I never thought I would celebrate over a R50 gift, but now here I was, longing for just R50 to buy tonight's tray of meat.

I really hoped I would be able to look back and laugh at all this one day. That's the other thing, you know. It's one thing to go through a difficult patch, but it's a complete other problem when your life simply turns around for the worst, and you never recover from it. What if nothing ever got better, and this became the rest of our lives? What if we continued to struggle to pay school fees, we never went on holiday again, and the kids lived a life riddled with struggles until their schooling days were done? Then they would actually long to leave the household and to break free into their own idea of financial freedom, vowing to never be as broke as their parents.

I know these thoughts were not exactly helping my situation, but they went through my mind a lot. I was desperate to be free. I longed for my old life, and when I was feeling somewhat positive, I dreamed of a miraculous turnaround, one in which my business had picked up and I was being invited to speak around the world, where I would take the family with me on international trips and take the children to Disney World. This gave me hope and a reason to wake up every morning.

Despite my erratic faith, I knew I was growing. I spent hours in prayer simply because tomorrow's bread, fuel for the car, and month-end payments depended desperately upon those prayers. My heart grew compassionate for those without. Suddenly, it was so important for me to give to others in my community, and I imagined what they were going through. How I wished I had something to share with those who had similar problems. And strangely, as I began to share my situation with others, I started to realize that there were many other families in situations similar to ours. I was truly amazed. I learned this one Sunday when I felt the urge to share with a friend and explain to her why we hadn't invited them over for lunch like we used to or even had the children over to play. I teared up as I began to explain our difficult situation to her. This showed me that I had not quite healed, and the pain of this season was still very real to me. She hugged me and took me totally by surprise when she said, "We are going through the exact same thing." She shared a little of her own situation, and I suddenly realized how difficult it must be for them. Then she shared that many other families in the church were going through the same thing. From that moment on, I firmly resolved to pray for all the other families in our communities who were going through similar problems. This realization gave me the courage to pray and confess the scriptures in place of my pity parties.

Probably the most significant beneficiaries of my difficult season were the security guards in our neighborhood. I had never had so much compassion for the less privileged as I had now, and each time I drove past our security gate, I felt their need in a way I had never experienced before. While I counted my coins in Pick 'n' Pay, I made a mental note to buy something for the security guards whenever I was in a position to do so. And that I did.

For the first time ever, I actually remembered the underprivileged and followed through with my good intentions. And the feeling of giving was too good not to share. I gave the food parcels to the children sitting in the back seat of my car, and they cheerfully handed these to the guards. The responses we received were enough to uplift my downcast heart. Giving felt better than any purchase I had ever made for myself, better than slipping my feet into a new pair of leather heels or trying on a new business suit. Had I really been missing out on all of this?

Stage 4: Baptism by Fire

Unfortunately, all of that fasting and prayer didn't render me immune to depression. Okay, so I wasn't exactly clinically depressed, but nonetheless, I had the blues, and I had them bad.

What are you really meant to do while you wait? I had done everything I knew to do. My profile was everywhere, complete with CV and cover letter. The website was still working, I tested my email weekly, and still nothing.

It didn't take me long to settle into a new routine. I would drive home on autopilot from the early morning school run, passively listening to the news station. So much was going on in South Africa, and it was comforting to get lost in the politics, to passively listen to the passionate assertions of radio callers, ordinary citizens like myself ranting about racism, protesting over dysfunctional schooling systems, or merely complaining about corrupt government officials. Listening to other people's issues felt like a welcome break from my own. But just as the discussions were becoming more entertaining, I would be jabbed back to reality as I parked my car outside the house.

Back at home, what on earth could I do with myself? There was nothing else, absolutely nothing, to do after eating breakfast, apart from going back to bed. So that was what I did, day in and day out. I would get back from the morning school drop-off, eat whatever was available for breakfast, and march myself back to bed. My intention was always to spend hours in prayer and reflection, but that barely lasted more than thirty minutes at a time. Before I knew it, I would be dozing off and would surrender myself to another couple of hours of escapist sleep.

This was almost always followed by an early lunch and then an hour or so of television before I dragged myself back to school to collect the kids. Months went on in this way, and I slowly withdrew into myself. I found the television a comforting escape since I could sit passively and disappear into someone else's world and forget my own. Hopefully, when I eventually woke up from escapism, my life would be changed, and I could start living again. So essentially, I was waiting for my miracle, waiting for an answer and for the open doors I needed to get my business to work.

One Friday, while I passively stood in my kitchen, partly cooking dinner and partly daydreaming, I had the bright idea to fill up the quiet hour with some passive entertainment while I cooked. Off I went to the television, where I promptly discovered that the T. D. Jakes show was on. I sat down to watch, and before long I was deeply engrossed in the discussion of the day and had blissfully forgotten about the dinner I was supposed to be cooking.

"Mommy, something's burning." Those words shook me out of my reverie, and I promptly remembered the last action I had made in the kitchen. My senses were functional again, and I could smell the intense stream of gray smoke penetrating the air in the lounge and dining room.

With an unexpected burst of energy, my jelly legs sprang me toward the kitchen, and before I could turn into the room, I heard it: the sound of air providing clean nourishment to the smoke stream. As I turned to enter the kitchen, there it was, a large orange flame, growing from the oil-filled pan right up to the extractor fan!

I remembered reading a report about myself a few years earlier. I had undergone an exhausting batch of psychometric tests in preparation for a promotion and was reading the fourteen-page report with all my personal findings. There it had been in black and white: "Valerie is likely to remain calm under extreme pressure." And my boss's words had reinforced this finding even further: "It doesn't matter what happens—the entire building could be on fire, and Val would be the most calm of us all."

I had tried to assure him that my calm appearance was just that, an appearance, and that I actually panicked like everyone else on the inside.

And here I was now, with a real house fire before my eyes and the danger of the situation slowly setting in on the inside.

My son, bless his heart, came rushing in after me to see what he could do to help, but I angrily ordered him to get out of the kitchen and go call Daddy.

I was thankful for the non-diplomacy of children at that time. The poor child fled off down the passage, yelling, "Daddy, Mommy's started a fire in the kitchen!"

So I may be blessed with the gift of remaining calm under pressure, but apparently, that does not automatically come with the added gift of thinking of intelligent practical steps to mitigate danger.

My husband really was a hero! He ran off and almost instantly was back with a blanket, which he swiftly laid on top of the blazing pan, and then he carried the entire smoky hazard out to the back garden. This was after ordering the children to stop spectating and go outside. Actually, he ordered both the children and me, but I was too busy opening up windows to prevent the furniture from absorbing the overwhelming clouds of black smoke that now filled the house.

At ten that night, we were still in casualty, or the emergency department, at the hospital. All of us had had our turn on the oxygen machine, and we were cleared and sent home after promising to come right back should any of us experience shortness of breath overnight.

I was physically and emotionally drained. We had to buy takeaway meals after all of that since there was no way of cooking. Was I really that detached and disturbed? How could I have honestly sat on the couch, leaving a pot of oil on the stove unattended? I finally admitted to myself that I had to wake up from my depressing reality and take the reins on my life again. In my despair, I had let go of everything, and I really wasn't myself any longer.

How would this affect the children? I remembered looking up during the fire as the clouds of thick gray smoke rose to the ceiling, staining the walls as they went. I was sure the house was on the brink of catching fire.

Was this what my life was becoming at the age of forty-one? I felt a deep sense of resignation at the thought of losing all of our assets and everything we had worked for up until now. Our financial situation was threatening some of our other properties, and now I was about to lose the roof over our heads to a fire.

I felt numb as I crawled into bed that night. I was exhausted. I prayed desperately for the strength to go on.

Stage 5: Gratitude

The feeling of complete attenuation that followed the fire soon led to an overwhelming sense of gratitude. We all could have died in that fire if we had reacted any slower or if just one factor had been different. With that realization came a sense of peace that I really had not expected.

My life was what it was, and nothing was going to change that except a true miracle. I had done a whole lot of things myself to change the situation this year, and they had not amounted to much. I felt like I was officially ready to resign to my situation and let go of the reins. There were so many parents who really had very little time to spend with their children, and here I was with all the time in the world to do so. I allowed myself to enjoy my time at home and even began to watch television once again. I cooked meals and enjoyed them and relaxed so much more than before.

Yes, I still wanted my business to pick up and become a booming success, but while it wasn't yet there, I was going to enjoy the journey. For the first time in a long time, I enjoyed being home and stopped living for the future. My focus became today and the opportunity that was today. What could I do today so that I mattered to my family and to others around me? What could I do today to make sure that I didn't look back and regret this day but that I was proud of who I was, the message I carried, and what I represented?

All of a sudden, my book-writing became a priority for me once again. I was able to use the time I had toward writing and didn't feel as though I was stealing from higher-priority activities. I helped the children organize their time to accommodate their homework and extramurals as well as theater activities that my daughter had become involved in. It was hugely rewarding, and I felt like I was adding value to my home, albeit on a shoestring budget. I realized that the excuses I had made for so long were in essence invalid and that many meaningful goals could be achieved with little or no money.

I also found that I was much more available for communicating and building relationships with family, particularly those who were in other countries, whom I often felt I never had the time to contact. Using various social media platforms, I managed to keep in touch with family and really connect on a deep level, which is important for me.

My entire outlook was changing. I didn't feel the need to constantly be sitting at my laptop, striving and trying to make things happen for myself. I had done this for the longest time, actually ever since my school days decades ago. So we didn't quite have laptops at that time, but I remember spending countless hours studying. I never really felt the pressure of studying, I must admit. It was a strange sort of pastime for me. I had gotten myself into the habit of whipping out my books and studying whenever I had some time, and I actually enjoyed doing it in social settings. So in my large family, while the rest of the family was busy chatting, laughing, dressing up, or even just relaxing, I found a safe place to sit in their presence and get into my books. It gave me a sense of being productive while still being present in social settings.

So for the first time in a very long time, I just lived. There was no pressure to produce or perform. I felt relieved. My husband played an important role in this season for me. As constant as the hills, he continued to reassure me that I didn't need to engineer anything or perform any miracles overnight. He was happy as long as I followed up on inquiries and responded to any interest I received either for training or for bookings in our holiday apartment.

There was so much to be grateful for. I had a husband who was working very hard to make sure we could maintain our lives on one salary, children who didn't make demands and who prayed with us for a breakthrough, a housekeeper who continued to work for us cheerfully despite the fact that she had not been paid in months, and friends and family who loved us and helped us in our time of trouble.

This mattered more than anything money could buy. And for the first time I realized it. I never lost my new perspective regarding the value of time. I watched many full-time employed moms and remembered my own days of driving around frantically to get from the office to the school in double-quick time, navigating what seemed to be impossible traffic and praying that by a miracle I would get to school on time and still make it to the extramural activity. I remember countless instances of sitting in traffic, watching the clock tick, and missing an appointment at the school or forfeiting an extramural lesson because there was just no way of getting out of the traffic jam I was in. I hated myself for it for the longest time. Suddenly, I realized that there was no amount of money that would make that situation acceptable to me any longer.

A SMALL CLOUD

The days and weeks that followed had me focused on administration around insurance claims and managing workmen who came in to clean up the ashes, replace the stove and extractor fan, and paint the walls and ceiling.

I had no idea why the fire had to happen, and by that stage I was tired of asking questions. Strangely, the newly painted walls had an uplifting effect on me, and I felt ready to give life another try.

I felt like it was a new season, and that it was. In a single week, my phone had started ringing, and I had been offered three facilitation opportunities for that month! Wow, that felt unbelievable! I could hardly wait to get there and get working! I busied myself with preparation and got all of my ducks in a row well before time. Preparing to get back to work again felt exhilarating. I remember texting my dad with the announcement of my three upcoming opportunities and wondering how absurd my excitement about it must seem, while at the same time feeling assured that he would truly be celebrating with me, having prayed for me over the past few months.

Suddenly, all of those months of moping and self-pity felt a little wasted, and I regretted the stay-at-home comfort-eating that meant I couldn't fit into some of my old business suits. I panicked and promptly got my body back to hard work—more focused early morning workouts and failed attempts at cutting down my food intake! For the first time in a long time, I felt uncomfortable with my size, and I prayed for the strength to control my appetite better. I remember having to go into a business school for a presentation. I had prepared my slides perfectly but had not spent adequate time thinking about what I would wear. At the last minute, I found myself rushing into my bedroom and trying frantically to pull up the pants of a beautiful formal suit, only to realize that they didn't fit any longer! What was I to do? I was literally between sizes. The size 8 pants that I was trying to squeeze into were squeezing the life out of my thighs, and the size 10 pants that were hanging in my cupboard were too big! So what did I do? I decided to go with the life-squeezing size 8 pants, and as I tried to button up, the button popped off the cloth. In my desperation, I grabbed a large safety pin and tried to hook both sides together and cover it up with my blouse and jacket. Thankfully, sanity prevailed, and I resorted to the larger size 10 pants, which I then rolled up around my waist, before running out of the house in time to make it to my presentation.

Nothing was going to stop me from making the most of the doors that opened up at this time. I was hugely grateful for every single opportunity, no matter how small, and I signed up for every facilitation date that I was offered. Work suddenly felt like a blessing to me again, and I don't remember ever feeling so appreciative for having work.

My phone was ringing again, and I had one standard answer to everything: "Yes!" With every open door, I could see groceries coming onto the dinner table again, fuel in my car, the maid being paid, and eventually, big things like school fees being paid! Wow, did it feel great to be back in business or what?

I made a point of showing up for every appointment at my very best, not only well-dressed and on time but also in a good mood and ready for a productive day of training and connecting.

I enjoyed the freedom of being able to facilitate for two or three days and have the next day free to attend concerts at the children's schools or just take a break at home or take a nap. Could this life be real? I was super-grateful and kept praying for even more open doors.

The more work I did, the more doors opened. They were opening everywhere, and I was getting busier and busier. All of a sudden, my phone calendar was becoming my favorite app as it kept me organized and perfectly scheduled for all of my commitments. I also had to become very comfortable with travel since some of my training bookings were outside of town, which meant I had to travel at least one night prior to training and spend a day or two away from home. With this came the need to organize the family even more precisely because lifts to school and extramurals needed to be pre-organized and managed so that the family continued to run smoothly in my absence.

I think for the most part I was incredulous. I literally went from taking long daily naps to going for days and sometimes weeks of busy travel and back-to-back facilitation. And the strangest thing is that I loved every moment of it. Yes, I missed the family when I traveled, but I was still so grateful for every open door and continued to pray for more.

With my idle days at home becoming fewer and fewer, I found I had less and less time to work on training materials, which was still a goal I had set in order to grow my business and be in a position to offer my own training in the future. This work became harder and harder to do since the times I was home were spent preparing invoices for past training and preparing myself for upcoming courses. How delightful it was to be home with the family over weekends. I was able to stop at the shop and spoil the children with a treat on the way home from school once again! Their looks of cheerful surprise when I offered treats were priceless! It automatically put the children in a good mood and set us up for a good evening.

I couldn't believe the privileges I had taken for granted before. My days of full-time employment had placed me in a financial position where I could spoil the kids when I wanted to, but unfortunately, my time had always been limited, and I was lucky if I could pick them up from school on any given day. My newfound entrepreneur lifestyle enabled me to have both ad hoc freedom and reasonable financial capacity, and this suited me perfectly. For the first time in a long time, I felt happy. I had been working toward feeling content for such a long time prior to this that I had written off any possibility of actually being happy with my life.

I tried hard not to forget the forgotten again now that my financial situation was changing. All of the security guards, car guards, and petrol attendants and the lowest earners in society who were just grateful to get a packet of rice or a loaf of bread—I couldn't forget them now. But the truth is that I found it increasingly easier to forget them. With the newfound elation of parking at the mall and buying most of what I needed and wanted without worrying about money, my head was now in a different space, and my concerns seemed to have shifted away from bare survival and toward choice—the choice of brand, the choice of how much I wanted to spend on a specific item, rather than having to settle on whatever was within reach financially on that particular day. All of that said, I could not dismiss the realization that I had walked a season in the shoes of the forgotten. Although I had quite frankly still had the privilege to be driving a luxury car during that season (albeit without fuel most of the time), I had nonetheless gained some appreciation of their struggle, which I was determined not to forget.

ROUNDTABLE
REFLECTIONS

S
o I was clearly stepping out of my closed world that consisted largely of my own needs and concerns and into the realm of "other." I knew this was right because it was essentially what my parents had been trying to teach me ever since my childhood. It was what society expected of every one of us. However, I was more than unprepared for the real lesson that was coming my way.

After joining the CEO Roundtable, chaired by Mike and Karen Cerff, I was in monthly contact with a group of local business owners much like myself, except that many of them had more business experience than I had, which meant that I learned a lot during our monthly workshops and looked forward to these gatherings more and more.

For one of our CEO Roundtable gatherings, Mike had invited a guest speaker, Dr. Chisango, who turned out to be a Zimbabwe-based evangelist and chairperson of the World Economic Congress (WEC). Dr. Chisango was given the platform to address our workshop early in our agenda, and he began by sharing a detailed story of how he had come to establish and chair the WEC. At the end of his story, Dr. Chisango commented, "Sometimes we need to allow people to abuse us in order for us to have influence and impact." I remember how I felt when I heard those words. Everything within me rejected that statement. My heart raced, and I felt my head begin to spin. I was itching to shoot my hand up and correct this man. Had he really come this far in life and in leadership without learning anything about self-management, emotional intelligence, and managing the expectations and demands of others? Surely, he should know something about setting, communicating, and managing boundaries. Why was he allowing people and whole communities to make demands on his time and resources without considering his own needs and entitlements to personal space and resources?

I breathed heavily as my heart continued to pound in my chest. As I waited for the most opportune moment to raise my hand, an overwhelming sense of calm came over me, and I felt myself giving up my impending battle. My heart was still racing, but instead of desperation to bring correction, I felt a deep wave of emotion coming over me. This man reminded me of my parents and their sacrifices, and this angered me. Why did I feel this way? I felt deeply uncomfortable and debated whether I should step out of the conference room to gather myself and breathe or continue to experience this. I now knew why I was angry, and I didn't quite know what to do about it.

Earlier in the year, I had finally accepted the reality that I was angry—angry with my parents for the kindness that they had demonstrated to our extended family and community while I was growing up. Some of these family and community members clearly had not deserved their kindness, and in fact, many of them had turned around and despised my parents. Why had my parents not realized that their strategy was not working? They had merely continued to show kindness to people. So many relatives, acquaintances, and mere strangers moved into our home for undetermined (and often extended) periods of time, and many of these people stayed and studied (at the expense of my parents), sought jobs for months on end, or merely used our home as a place of rest and refuge to recover and recuperate from various ailments. Reading this, I am sure you are able to appreciate the essence of my parents' hearts of kindness and generosity. I would too if I were but a reader of these words. However, living in the household presented a unique childhood experience, and this formed the basis of a particular mindset growing up.

I decided to do a quick mental count of the number of people my parents had accommodated during my childhood. By people they "accommodated," I mean those people who stayed inside our house for weeks at a time and at least once during my childhood. This included all of the cousins who were dropped off for school holidays for three or four weeks at a time (and there were often at least four cousins visiting at any one time). Also included were sick elderly aunts and uncles, young job-seeking cousins, and aspiring students who were in desperate need of funding.

My quick head count got me to thirty-eight, and I stopped out of mere shock and disbelief. So there it was. Growing up, I had lived in a household where at least thirty-eight relatives had at some stage or another stayed or lived with us. So pardon me if I was just a little bit careless about the kindness and generosity of my Good Samaritan parents.

Without dwelling on the impact of this situation, I realize that I need to make peace with this rather unique aspect of my past, and I am really yearning for an increased appreciation of my parents' sacrifices. I am also aware of the sense of resentment that I feel at having had to share my home with so many people without having had a say in the matter. The community in which we were raised expected this from people like my parents—people who had been able to rise above the difficult circumstances of being African people in pre-independent Zimbabwe—and it was not the degree to which one was able to do this that mattered, but the fact that one was no longer considered to be struggling as much as the rest. They were obligated to help others, and that was what they did. The impact that this might have had on their immediate family or children would have been considered a first-world problem and was therefore not a priority.

So back to the CEO Roundtable. My heart was still racing, and my hands were trembling now too. I had a lump in my throat and finally gave in to leaving the room for self-composure. As I walked to the restroom, I fought back the tears that welled up in my eyes and breathed in deeply. It was very selfish to be angry with people who made demands in an unequal society like Africa. I was selfish and spoiled and needed to get over myself. Why was I angry anyway? Hadn't I received an excellent education and attended the best universities? I had been deprived of nothing, and yet I was angry and resentful! I scolded myself all the way to the bathroom. I knew my parents loved me; I had no doubt about it. They had made it work. They had been able to accommodate everyone while looking after their own children. I just couldn't help wondering what life would have been like if we had just lived our own lives and if they had focused on us and our needs solely. I remembered how I had applied for boarding in my lower sixth year. I really wanted to get out of the house and focus on my studies and on athletics. I had made the athletic team, and there was early morning training at five thirty every day. At the time, Dad had committed himself to driving me to school, and we left the house at 5:15 a.m. every Tuesday and Thursday. I had spoken to the athletics coach, who was also conveniently the head of the hostel, and communicated my desire to move to the hostel. The boarders were getting a solid two hours of exam preparation study after daily homework, and I still had the hassle of getting home and helping with the cooking and then with washing up before starting homework at 8:00 p.m. I didn't finish with homework until ten o'clock and was exhausted by the time I began exam revision.

My application was to no avail. The fees the school was charging for boarding were impossible, and there was no way that Dad would have been able to pay them. It would have been unreasonable for me to insist on it.

So I spent my last school years trying to create a mental space in which I could think and work. I did this pretty well. I was able to escape to a place in my mind where I could engage with my learning content and disengage from my environment pretty well. The house was always buzzing with people talking, the television playing, and other household noises. I was expected to help with household duties to a significant extent and could not always just hide behind my books. I learned quite early in my schooling life that the wee hours of the morning were the best time to study. I asked my dad to be my daily alarm clock and to wake me up at two thirty each morning. He did this religiously, and I learned to respond quickly when he knocked on my door at this time each weekday. This really helped me set a habit for regular study. I could fit in two and half hours of study before going back to sleep at 5:00 a.m. for one more hour of sleep before the official 6:00 a.m. wake-up time.

I was exhausted that evening after the roundtable. As I drove home, my mind played back many memories of growing up in our family home. Many of the memories were very happy, and I cherished them. Like any introvert, I wished I could have had more personal space to get away from the noise and reflect. Nonetheless, this took nothing away from what I had had. I was grateful for my parents, and I was proud of them. In a way, I was slightly ashamed for having been angry with them for so long, but I gave myself the grace to acknowledge my anger as valid and to move past it. What a childhood that had been. I was pretty sure my parents had not planned to live like that, and I was aware of some of the disappointment they had experienced after many of those they had helped had either never been thankful for the opportunity or had simply resented them for not giving them even more.

I continued to reflect as I lay in bed that night. I weighed the options that my parents had had and realized that rather than choosing the easy way of enjoying their privilege and minding their own business, they had chosen to open up their doors and put up with the many attitudes, personalities, and preferences of the scores of people who arrived at our doorstep seeking help or hospitality in some form or other. This was the road less traveled, and there was nothing easy about it. It would have been so easy for them to throw in the towel and create a set of rules about who qualified for their assistance, how long they were welcome, and how they were expected to pay it back or pass it on. But they had chosen not to do this.

AFFLUENT ACTUALIZING

O ur good Dr. Chisango was becoming a regular visitor at our CEO Roundtable—and a very welcome visitor too. It never ceased to amaze me how he was able to inspire such a different perspective on what ordinarily would have appeared to be everyday life issues. He spoke about the daily challenges that he faced as a leader in rural Zimbabwe, and I wondered how he did not just give up and move to a more functional economy. I came to realize how many times I opted for the easy way out and didn't hang around for situations that seemed either too difficult or unnecessarily inconvenient.

Dr. Chisango spoke about the dangers of the untransformed city. He illustrated this with a biblical analogy of Jacob and his tent. Jacob moved to a new land with his children and looked after them and provided for them as best he could in his tent. As Jacob's children grew, however, they explored their surrounding communities, as any other teenagers would, and went into the city center to socialize with the local people of their new community. It was here where Jacob's daughters were defiled by the young men of the community. The learning point—we cannot prosper if we are the only ones thriving in our communities.

How strangely this teaching landed with me! I thought about all I had been accustomed to since childhood. Wherever we had lived, there always had been unemployed people and those who were struggling to make a living. Occasionally, we assisted them, but it wasn't the norm; they were there and would always be there. That is what we had come to know and live with.

And besides, there was never anything left to give to anyone. I had worked for over a decade, and it just seemed to me that the longer I worked, the more my "needs" list grew, which meant that my annual increases and my bonuses were already accounted for before they reached my bank account. First, it was just my husband and I when we were starting out. Like any other young couple, we dreamed of buying our own property, upgrading our car, and just settling into normal Johannesburg life.

Then a couple of years down the line, we had our son, and nineteen months thereafter, our daughter was born, and we had the pressures of early parenthood to worry about—baby room decorating, nappies, baby food, and eventually preschools. It feels like the demands are astronomical for parents at this time, and we can't imagine what would happen if any more demands came along. As it happens, the next phase actually does demand more from us financially, but thanks to a good education and the opportunities presented to graduates by corporate South Africa, we are in fact earning more by then, and of course, we opt for the most expensive schools, after careful research. And the pressures just continue to grow. Before we know it, we are up to our ears in "good debt" (a term coined by banks, no doubt), and one half of the happy couple is entertaining thoughts of opting out of the rat race. Now we have all the basic needs—shelter, food, a place to belong, and self-esteem emanating from career and personal development—and most likely, at least one partner is wondering if there isn't anything more than this. In our relationship, this was me. I eventually grew tired of waking up and going to work, day in and day out, and having only my salary (that's what it felt like at the time) to show for it. And even that was perfectly and wholly allocated to a monthly budget, which meant that before the digits hit my bank account, every cent was committed toward an essential aspect of running the household. I eventually woke up to the scary realization that I was trapped, trapped into the curse of waking up at five and dropping off children to school before facing the overwhelming traffic that characterized my route to work. The higher up I was promoted in the company, the more taxing my daily challenges became, until I downright dreaded my daily trip to the office. Long working days turned into weeks and weeks separated by weekends that seemed to be fewer and fewer. Saturdays were never long enough, and before I knew it, it was the dreaded Sunday night (thanks to television program *Carte Blanche* for reminding us religiously that another dreaded week at the office awaited us on the other side of Sunday night). And so it began all over again with a new week.

As any socially competent woman would do, I began to inquire with other women as to how they were coping with the hustle and bustle of life in Johannesburg and whether there really was more to life than this as far as they were concerned. And so the discussions began. To work or not to work, that was the question. With a couple of young children and a household that needed nurturing and organizing (and yes, of course, finances to run on), was the answer to be found in climbing the corporate ladder and pushing the boundaries of earning potential or opting out of the madness to provide something more than mere money to the members of the household? We all agreed it was a tough choice, and that's about all we really agreed upon as far as this topic was concerned. I watched some of my peers steel themselves to the emotional tugs of children and focus on growing their careers, mostly in corporations that placed little value on family, beyond the annual Christmas family fun day. They seemed to continue to thrive financially, affording the best schools, quality toys, and other gadgets of affluence, while those who opted out seemed to become fixated on "downsizing." They downsized at every level. Some sold their houses and bought smaller homes in less affluent suburbs (I knew I wasn't about to do that). They seemed to become experts in smart shopping and bargain hunting (which I loved), and the really radical ones began to homeschool their children. My world seemed to be growing, with all of these exciting debates living themselves out right before my eyes. In the world in which I had grown up, there had been no such thing as homeschooling. But all of a sudden, I knew a handful of women who had opted out to homeschool. And why not? Most of us were university-educated and very bright and resourceful women who loved our children. Why in the world hadn't this practice been more widespread before?

I was excited about the dynamism of this season of my life and the apparent options that were presenting themselves. But that certainly did not eliminate the fear I felt of walking away from a regular monthly salary (particularly a salary of the proportions that I had become used to). How on earth do you live and plan, and what do you have to look forward to, without that predictable text message from the bank arriving like clockwork on the eve of the twenty-fifth of the month, guaranteeing the continuity of your security and providing the green light for an enjoyable and comfortable residential status in one of the most affluent cities in the world?

So for me, the debate continued. And true to my introverted nature, I delved into further research on the topic. I read papers and magazine articles and tuned into every television or radio program where the issue was discussed. I had been fortunate enough to restructure my workday somewhat, to free myself up to do the daily school run at the end of the children's school day. Previously, I had had to hire a "school mom," who was in fact a stay-at-home mom who was prepared to perform the task for me in exchange for some much-needed income. This had worked out wonderfully since she was a warm and kind lady whom the children simply adored. It certainly had taken away the stress of worrying about the children having to be in aftercare until I finished work and then the additional stress of worrying about whether traffic would be kind enough to let me get to the school before aftercare was officially over. A number of times, I had arrived late and found my two were the last to be collected, which made me feel completely rotten and a failure. So finding someone to help me with my precious bundles had been superb! The arrangement had worked beautifully until one day when I was strolling on the school campus with the children, after collecting them from their respective classes. I had taken a day of leave from work and was enjoying the pleasurable experience of collecting the children myself, having canceled my school mom for the day.

"Oh, are these your children?" I will never forget those words. I had noticed a familiar face and waved at the woman, another school mom, walking toward me, and she had returned the gesture with those dreaded words. I had just barely uttered a response, confirming they were indeed my children, when she retorted, "Oh, that's nice. I always see them with a blonde lady, and I assumed they were adopted!"

At that stage, I was grateful that both my children were too young to understand the complexity of those words! I mean, really, and the lack of tact! I felt attenuated! Even if she had thought that, wasn't it rather rude to actually say that to a mother?

Anyway, that woman's outburst was enough to set my next goal. I had to collect my own children from school and had to find a way to make that happen as soon as possible. Soon thereafter, I was headhunted for a job that was slightly closer to home. My first point of negotiation with my new manager was that I pop out between 12:00 and 2:00 p.m. to collect my children and drop them off at home before returning to work for the afternoon. That meant I had to stay in the office a little later than everyone else, but I was content knowing the children were in the safety of our home and not waiting at aftercare or being mistaken for someone else's children.

It wasn't long after that that I successfully requested a change in working hours toward a half-day arrangement. It was quite a surprise to my manager, but he was fair enough to suggest that my request be tabled at the executives' meeting and that I prepare a proposal.

Not really knowing where to begin, I sat down and put finger to laptop. I articulated the difficult situation in which I found myself and emphasized my moral and motherly responsibility to tend to my young children while continuing to participate productively in the work of the organization. Thankfully, my impassioned plea was given the stamp of approval, and there I was in the envied position of holding a management role and working half of the day on a reduced income. To be quite honest, I was more than happy to take the salary reduction if it meant being home with my children during afternoons, and I made sure that my mobile phone was always on and that I dared not miss a call from the office during those afternoons. That was fair enough.

Looking back, I had the social advances of Australia and New Zealand to thank for this success. Having done some research on the plight of women in management throughout the world, I was aware that some of these more innovative working arrangements were alive and well in these countries, and it certainly helped that our company's chief executive officer held a doctorate in organizational development.

CHARITIES AND RECITALS

B ack to the present, here I was in 2017, class mom–cum–entrepreneur. Because things had been rather quiet on the business front, I had time on my hands to focus on "class-momming," which was a career that actually had chosen me and not the other way round.

My daughter had moved to a prestigious new school (as a result of an unexpected scholarship), and during one of my morning drop-offs and quick hallos with the teacher, there was a brief conversation about one of the mothers in the class who had recently undergone surgery. The teacher asked if I wouldn't mind picking up a bunch of flowers and delivering them to the dear family on behalf of the class. Of course, how could I mind that? I would certainly appreciate this kind gesture if I were in this mom's position. And would I mind picking up a lasagna or something for dinner for the precious family? Absolutely, not a problem!

After my good turn, the lovely teacher (bless her heart) gave me a list of parents' names and contact details and suggested that I open a WhatsApp group to facilitate communication between the school and the parents. And that is how I came to acquire the title "class mom."

Having not quite figured out this new bunch of parents, I had made the assumption (from the mere magnitude of the school fees) that most if not all parents would be employed full-time, so I had heavenly visions of a very quiet WhatsApp group with one or two key players, since many of these busy and hardworking professionals likely would not enjoy being disturbed with regular pings about school requirements, extramural schedules, and class outings.

And oh, how wrong was my assumption! I soon came to the awakening that my new school community consisted of a mixture of high-profile executives and business owners whose partners were either working from home (in some capacity or another) or committed to the running of a household full-time. So in a nutshell, my new WhatsApp group consisted of fully engaged, highly intelligent, and organized people! If you have ever been an administrator on a WhatsApp group, you will agree that this is probably the worst kind of membership profile you can get, particularly if you were hoping for some peace and quiet.

Thankfully, my lack of consistent gainful employment meant that I had the time and mental space to plan and deliver meaningful and regular communication in the group. The class teacher was amazing at providing me with updates, and between us we kept the grade 4 class running like a well-oiled machine.

Before long, however, my newfound teacher friend expressed her desire to initiate fundraising efforts for the surrounding communities. I felt completely panicked! It was bad enough that I had succumbed to the idea of being class mom for the year, but I simply could not venture further into the deep end than I had already. My fundraising experience had consisted purely of watching other people raise funds and occasionally supporting these efforts through buying goods or contributing to merchandise. But there was no need to panic! To my absolute pleasure, as soon as I put a call on the WhatsApp group for assistance, I received a number of responses from available mothers, among them a wonder woman we came to know as our "fundraising queen." Thereafter, my life as a class mom became a series of class get-togethers (which I coordinated with the help of an amazing "executive committee" that self-formed in preparation for the first event) and a number of hot dog sales, cake and cool drink sales, and other innovative events through which to raise funds for abandoned animals, underprivileged communities, and less fortunate schools in our surrounding area. All of these activities gained grade 4 a fast-growing reputation for being the most active class in the new school and won us the "giving back" award for exemplifying the school's motto ("we shall give back").

In between charity events and family get-togethers, I attended numerous musical recitals with other mothers who also seemed to have copious amounts of time on their hands. Our new school had the most exquisite facilities, including a manor house with state-of-the-art musical, dance, and drama facilities, as well as beautifully furnished open areas where parents were welcome to relax and chat or catch up on work while waiting for afternoon pickups.

For most of the time, I wondered if this was real. Could one really have access to this and have the time to enjoy it? The world I had come to know had taught me that I had to choose either time or money. How did these parents do it? Who was paying for this world-class educational opportunity while we all lay back, sipping coffee and cooing over our young performers? The experience gave me a real appreciation of the amount of money that some families were making in Johannesburg. Was it really possible for one young family to have made enough money to send three of their four children to an international school such as this? After doing a few mental calculations to determine the hefty sum of money it would cost the family and having considered the earning potential of two professional parents, I concluded that there must be some form of inheritance involved; that was the only plausible explanation. Either my husband and I had been doing something very wrong, or I had merely underestimated the extent of generational wealth that had been passed down familial lines over the centuries.

Nonetheless, here I was, sipping coffee with the who's who of the city. Thanks to my private girls' school experience, I was well-equipped with the necessary social etiquette to mingle and fit in. It felt a little like sitting by the fire with your favorite fairy tale—not a short ten-minute fairy tale, but one of those really thick editions written in old England—and getting so lost in the tale that you blink and find yourself at a ball with all of the most prominent families of the era. You are tempted to sit back and watch but then realize you are actually there, and everyone knows who you are! How glorious!

A "FISHY" PROPOSAL

I t was a warm Friday morning, and I had just parked my car at a business school, ready for a meeting that would begin in the next twenty minutes. I intended on using the next few minutes to catch up on phone calls and emails and was just firing up my laptop when my phone began to vibrate. The number on the screen was unknown to me, and I assumed the call was from a telesales company.

I nevertheless answered the call professionally (you never know when a potential client might be on the other end), and I was greeted by a recruitment agent, a young man who later shared with me that he had grown up in the United Kingdom and later relocated to South Africa.

Like any good recruitment agent, he began by asking me if I was still on the job market. I said no and informed him that I was on the market for short-term consulting work. He then asked if I would mind if he told me of the position that he was calling about all the same. I agreed (and would regret that decision for months).

The position was almost identical to my previous corporate executive position and had two significant points of interest for me. It was based in East London (oh, how I romanticized life on the coast), and it was offering a more handsome salary than my previous corporate pay.

My heart began to race almost immediately, and after speaking to the young gentleman, I made a call to my husband, hoping that he would point out all the reasons why this would never work and why it would be a bad idea.

Instead, he listened intently as I retold the highlights of the position, and thereafter, he exclaimed, "We're moving to the coast!"

Now I could hear my heart thumping in my chest and ears, and my mind was in overdrive. I envisioned a beautiful family home by the beach, where my family would spend some lazy weekends fishing and taking walks on the beach. I would work in East London, a small town where the driving time from home to the office would be approximately eighteen minutes (thanks to the GPS app) and where the cost of living was lower than in Johannesburg. Moreover, on the proposed salary, my husband would be able to take some time off until he found a lucrative business venture in the industrial development zone, and our lives would be slower and happier than what they were currently in Johannesburg.

My reverie went on and on for first a few days and then a full two weeks. I gave the agent permission to submit my résumé for the post, and meanwhile, I researched everything (and I mean everything) there was to be found out about life on the coast. I identified possible schools for the children as well as a couple of potential suburbs in which we could buy a house. The location had to be close enough to the beach to provide the coastal town feel as well as reasonably close to my office and the children's schools. We would buy a good four-wheel-drive vehicle that would enable us to do holidays well, and the fuel consumption would definitely not be a problem on the executive salary that I was lined up for. I swung in and out of worry about going back to work but periodically found solace in the fact that the job was in a very small dot of a coastal town where nothing happened after 4:00 p.m. on a weekday. Weekends would be for my family and me, and I had already identified a couple of good churches in the area.

However, as the weeks wore on and my business kept me busy, I soon forgot about the possibility of East London. I was enjoying facilitating and traveling and meeting and impacting people. My phone was ringing more frequently than ever before, and I was grateful for the breakthrough. So as you might imagine, I was somewhat freaked out to receive a call from my young gentleman recruitment agent, who left me a voice message informing me of an interview in East London!

I was truly horrified! I mean, it was one thing to fantasize about moving to the coast to start a new, slower life, back at work in a sensible town, but it was a complete other thing to actually do it!

I felt the interview was a step closer to a life that I really was not ready for. How could I leave a business that I had just begun, that was just starting to thrive in the business capital of the country? And how on earth could I move the children, at this impressionable age, to a near-dead town, away from the possibility of theater shows and miles away from the high schools they had their eyes on?

This kicked off another few weeks of worry. Fortunately, I was so booked up with facilitation appointments over the few weeks that followed that I could not make a face-to-face interview, and the employer suggested that we schedule a Skype call within the next few weeks.

As it turned out, however, the face-to-face interviews ran overtime, and there was no time left for the interview panel to conduct the Skype interview, so I escaped the temptation of a coastal life and an executive full-time position.

I felt an inexplicable sense of relief. I felt as though I had been afforded a new lease on my business and that I could now throw myself fully into making this business a success. The temptation to go back to full-time work continues to rear its ugly head occasionally, particularly when finances are tight and pressure for a more regular income mounts.

I remember taking the poll to the children during the East

London temptation season. "How would you feel about Mommy going back to work?" And the answer was always the same. They felt that I owed it to myself to give the business a chance—that was particularly the reply of my oldest, my son. My daughter was always very clear about her need for my time. She enjoyed the fact that when I was not working, I could attend her school functions and music concerts; this meant a lot to her.

I guess there is no recipe when it comes to these things. Some things will work for your family, and some won't. And as for moving, I knew that would never really go down well with them. My son was very generous about it and agreed to prioritize the interests of the family as a whole. My daughter, on the other hand, was very clear that she was fully opposed to the idea and had no intentions of leaving her international school and scholarship, which in all fairness was understandable.

In addition to the relief I felt about sticking to my business, I equally felt a sense of relief about avoiding organizational politics and avoiding the inflexibility of having to be somewhere at eight o'clock every morning and not being released until four in the afternoon. This was something that I really would have struggled with, considering how I currently manage my days. On non-working days, my time is my own, and I can decide to attend children's school functions, do my weekly grocery shopping, and work out at the gym when it is convenient. I have become accustomed to being my own boss to a large extent and am grateful for that. Squeezing in ad hoc work assignments late into the evening doesn't bother me if it means freeing up an afternoon to prioritize family, friends, or health.

So it was goodbye to East London, and what a relief that was! I had secretly feared having to live in a small town with a limited number of coffee shops (yes, that matters), where I would feel completely overdressed for wearing makeup and would not even need to drive on the highway. Yes, we humans are complex. We don't always know what we actually want, do we?

GOING HOME

The further the year wore on, the more my heart longed for home—but not home as I had come to know it, my South African suburban neighborhood where I hardly knew my neighbors and life felt like a bit of a nonstop treadmill. I was aching to go back to the land of my fathers, where I was born and had spent my childhood. I found myself wondering about Zimbabwe a lot. I wondered how my parents were really getting on with life (aside from the bits of information I gathered from WhatsApp messages and brief telephone conversations). I thought about my cousins, many of whom I had been very close to growing up. How were they coping with life in Zimbabwe, with the stresses of unemployment and the pressures to provide for families in spite of the difficulties?

I articulated my heart's pain to my husband, and he was initially rather quick to diagnose my problem. His suggestion was that I needed to build my own culture and community right here in Johannesburg and start creating a heritage for myself and my children as opposed to longing for a time and place that were long gone. I can't honestly say that I even tried to entertain that suggestion. For starters, I was living in Johannesburg, where I could count the number of family members on one hand, so that wasn't going to work. And besides that, the family whom I knew in Johannesburg had become Johannesburgers themselves. They were busy people who slogged from eight to six on weekdays and hibernated most of the weekend, like many of us were accustomed to in this busy city.

And quite frankly, I felt that my heart's cry had not been heard. I wanted to go home. I wanted to be back in our old house, in my mother's kitchen, cooking, eating, laughing, and sitting out in the sun, chatting endlessly, not caring what time it was and having no agenda and no routine. I wanted to go back for another taste of the good ole days. That's what I really wanted.

After days of repeating my frustrations with the pace of Johannesburg life and my overwhelming need for a real African break, I got the green light, and within weeks, flights were booked, and plans were made for a real Zimbabwean Christmas! Look out, Harare—here I come!

It's amazing how things seem to shrink as you grow up and leave your hometown and experience the world. Each time I have gone back home, my mind has struggled to grasp the lack of magnitude of Harare and, in fact, of Zimbabwe. Everything seems minute and micro-scaled compared to the massive scale of global industries in South Africa. The lack of an actual highway is glaring, and the city really feels like a dot.

It was the evening of December 11 when we stepped off the plane, having landed in Harare just after nine o'clock. The airport had been renovated, but wow, it still looked so very small. I had to quickly repent of the arrogance with which I had considered the airport in Lesotho when I had traveled there for business just a week ago. I had frowned upon its lack of size and stature, and here I was, home at my own home airport, and it really did not fare that much better.

Nonetheless, being home felt like a breath of fresh air. I had flown up with the children, and my husband would follow a week later with the car. We were greeted in Shona by a very pleasant gentleman at immigration, who welcomed the children to Zimbabwe and gave us a generous number of visiting days so we could enjoy Christmas with the grandparents. I felt immediately uplifted as we walked through customs and spotted both my brother and my sister waiting for us on the other side! How glorious to be home at last! I immediately forgot to worry about crime and the possibility of being hijacked or followed home from the airport. I was home, and nothing else mattered for now.

The next morning, I was adamant not to give up my exercise priority and began my day with a walk with Dad, just like during university holidays. I used to look forward to taking walks with my father and chatting about anything and everything. This time we had the children, who happily tagged along, and what an enjoyable time it was. My old neighborhood was well transformed, with new houses having sprung up all over as well as a couple of schools. It was all so encouraging. Zimbabwe was becoming an option again, and my heart felt uplifted. For the longest time, I would come home and have to deal with a real sense of depression at the state of my parents' house, the state of the neighborhood, and the state of the nation as a whole. This time, the house was still cracking and in a bad state, but there was hope. A number of property developers were in serious negotiations with my parents, and the evidence of their workmanship was springing up all over the neighborhood. On the streets, citizens were upbeat and spoke freely, for the first time ever, expressing political views that had always been taboo. It was the best time to be home.

The following week saw my husband's arrival in Harare to a very warm Zimbabwean welcome. He came laden with litchis and scones (true Venda gifts), which brought even more festivity to his homecoming! His arrival was followed by the arrival of my brother (also from Johannesburg) and my cousin from England, and soon the house was alive and full of screaming grandchildren, chatting grown-ups, and laughter. The evenings were very special. After putting the grandchildren to bed, we sat around the dining room table with coffee and cake and biscuits (whatever one could find) and chatted and laughed until midnight! Morning did not begin until after nine o'clock, so that worked very well!

It wasn't long before my mind began to consider the real opportunity that Zimbabwe seemed to present. My home country had always held a special place in my heart, and I wondered whether it would be possible to offer some of my training and coaching services here. The people really seemed to be hungry for growth and development, which was nothing new; I had been brought up that way too. Education had always been the answer to our problems, and it was an unspoken priority throughout the land, wherever one went. Due to years of instability and difficult politics in Zimbabwe, the country had fallen behind in development terms, and there seemed to be a visible lag in advancement in the business arena (as well as many other areas). Work had been a rare and uncommon blessing, which meant that thousands of educated professionals had had no other choice but to settle for running struggling home-based businesses with minimal profit margins or to simply accept unskilled laborer work and archive their university degrees.

So I felt a strong attraction to this precious population, but I really wasn't sure where to begin. I knew very little about the working environment in Zimbabwe. After all, I had finished high school and left for university at the age of nineteen and had really only been home for university vacations and the longer one-year break between my honors and master's degrees. I was aware, though, of the stark differences between the working cultures of Zimbabwe and South Africa (specifically our fast-paced Johannesburg). I had learned over the years through some of my friends who had experienced working life in Zimbabwe how difficult it had been for them to transition from corporate Zimbabwe, where morning greetings could take up to half an hour as colleagues inquired after the well-being of your family (with unique sincerity) before settling into the day's work. That is not something we find much of in Johannesburg. If one does receive a greeting in the morning, it is a very rushed "How you doing?" to which the response is "Fine, an' you?"—which really often leaves one wondering whether the person actually saw you, let alone heard you.

When I really could no longer hold back, I began my face-to-face marketing efforts. I made calls and sent emails in an effort to just let people know I was out there and how much I was longing to partner with local companies to develop employees and grow businesses.

And before long, the most interesting of doors swung open. I was offered a radio interview on one of the local radio stations to speak on one of my pet loves: leadership development and emotional intelligence. I must say, I was rather surprised by how readily I accepted the invitation and by my apparent lack of nervousness at the prospect of being interviewed on radio for the very first time. I think I was mostly incredulous and extremely grateful for the opportunity, so I kind of forgot to be nervous. In fact, I hardly had time to work up my nerves since I received the invitation at 8:00 p.m. for a 9:00 a.m. interview the following day!

The radio interview turned out to be a significant milestone in my entrepreneurial journey. I found myself wearing earphones and sitting opposite a radio presenter, answering his questions, laughing at his jokes, and interestedly engaging with the messages sent by listeners. In a nutshell I loved it! Moreover, it seemed to give my parents a better understanding of the business I was launching. What a sense of pride I felt when my mom commented that she and Dad had listened to my interview and exclaimed, "Is this really our daughter?"

I think that was enough for me. It was important to put myself out there and moreover to get my parents' buy-in.

ANOTHER SOB AND
THEN A SIGH

The remainder of my time at home was a memorable collage of long days spent chatting with family members and playing with nieces and nephews, all flowing into each other. Good food was cooked in my mom's kitchen, and we enjoyed long conversations at meal tables, which turned into coffees and desserts, decorated by laughs and sighs and longings for all of this to never end.

Everyone was home with the exception of my sister who lived in New Zealand. In more ways than one, she had really been the lifesaver of the family, making sure that our parents were well provided for and that all the children in the family were taken care of and spoiled to some extent and just loving on so many of us in different ways. She was on the brink of purchasing a new home and starting a new job and therefore couldn't join us for Christmas this time.

We thought about her a lot and laughed at childhood memories. There were so many memories that made us laugh and cry at the same time. What a joy it was to watch my own children play with my brother's children and have the occasional fights that just sealed the brotherly relationships. I felt more blessed than ever before. There was no amount of money that could buy that, and for the first time in a long time, we all realized how rich we were as a family. We had been to many functions hosted by families who were financially much better off than we were, but we could say in confidence that we were the richest of them all. Mom and Dad were still together, and they loved all of us, and they were basking in the joy of having so many of us under their roof all at the same time. Yes, their house was cracking and needed to be demolished and rebuilt, and yes, they had been through times of lack, and a number of us were still trying to establish businesses, but we would have traded everything to keep the unity and the love that was in our home.

But inevitably, with each memorable day came the realization that soon we would be leaving and heading back to our home country of South Africa. In some ways I missed South Africa, but I so wanted all of this to carry on and to just savor the warmth of relationships and the good times.

So as usual departing was difficult. I stopped counting the number of times I hugged Mom and Dad and said goodbye. There was always something or other that had been forgotten or some other reason to delay our takeoff.

Finally, we hit the road. I was teary-eyed after saying goodbye to my sister, who was headed back to Namibia with her husband. I knew it might be long before I would see her again too.

As usual, I felt exhausted as we set off. I was grateful that my husband was driving, and I could just get lost in my head and my heart. I prayed silently that I would see my parents and the entire family again, and before long the hum of the car had lulled me to sleep.

The border was disorderly as usual. There were many Zimbabweans walking purposefully between official buildings, carrying passports and luggage and hoping that nothing would stop them from crossing over to the possibility of work and income and a livelihood in South Africa. Zimbabwe promised many opportunities at that moment in time, but the reality was that it would take some time for all the optimism to manifest into actual jobs, income, and a decent quality of life.

So the rat race continued. Officials watched queues of people and served one at a time, questioning intent, scrutinizing documents, and exercising discretion in their issuing of dates and extensions.

True to form, the language factor became our most valuable asset as soon as we entered the immigration office, as my husband greeted the officials in Venda. Almost like magic, we were ushered to the front of the queue, our passports were stamped, and we were sent off with well-wishes back into our South Africa.

As our car drove slowly across the Limpopo bridge, I felt a dull ache in my heart. I was back home in South Africa. I had honestly stopped trying to make sense of which of these two nations was truly home for me. My heart belonged to both nations, and I was a foreigner in neither one.

I thought about Mom and Dad and all of the family members I had left behind, and the ache deepened. I swallowed another muffled sob as we reached the end of the bridge. I was home now, and these were my people too. The children breathed an excited sigh of relief as we hit the South African highways. I could tell they had missed this beautifully developed land that was their home. We were surrounded by concrete, state-of-the-art fuel stations, and even a new mall. *Here we go again*, I thought. I sighed.

We stopped over at the new mall and couldn't resist referring to merchandise value in dollars. We had so quickly become accustomed to Zimbabwe's borrowed US dollar currency, and now everything seemed to be evaluated in dollars. Of course, this gave us a newfound respect for the cost of living in South Africa as opposed to Zimbabwe. Everything seemed to be so cheap all of a sudden, and we were relieved that we didn't have to try to make a living in Zimbabwe.

After a quick meal stop, we headed for my husband's parents' village, and it was dark when we finally arrived. I felt like I was seeing it for the very first time.

My visit home seemed to have had a significant impact on my self-concept. I felt like I was someone new, and for the first time in a very long time, I was sure of where I was and where I was going, and I knew I was loved and valued. Going home did that for me. I now understood the overwhelming longing I had felt for months prior to going home. I had wanted to see my people, understand my heritage, and find myself somewhere along the lineage and the culture.

This had happened for me, and I could feel it. I also felt empowered, more than I had ever felt before. I was at home, I was powerful, and it was my mission to be an agent for change. How could life be better (even if it was for just one person) because I was here? I was grateful for the new perspective, and I felt ready for 2018.

This year was going to be big. There was no time to waste, and I wasn't getting any younger. This year was my time to do everything I could to grow the business I had been dreaming of over the past decade. I was sure that I wanted to embark on my doctoral studies in 2019, which meant that 2018 was the only chance I had to throw myself fully into my business and my calling. I was going to make it count in every way possible.

HOPE DEFERRED (AGAIN)

T he year got off to a fast start with a number of facilitation dates confirmed in January, which meant that my calendar for the end of January and February was well-populated by the middle of January. This gave me a great sense of comfort and reassurance about paying the bills and keeping us out of trouble financially.

I had finally recovered from last year's difficulties and stress, and all I wanted to do was put it all behind me and move on. I remembered all of those hard months when I had brought in no income whatsoever and spent hours and days crying in the car, wondering how we were going to pay the mortgage, fill up the car to take the children to school, and do a decent amount of grocery shopping. Grocery shopping had become a distant memory for me months ago. I couldn't remember when last we had visited a store and stocked up on provisions like I used to do in my employed days. I longed for the chance to do that again, to just walk down the store aisles, picking and choosing what I desired without worrying about the bill.

My busy February was a great blessing for me, even though I discovered that I had a foot condition that required physiotherapy once per week. I was still so grateful that I could continue to work in spite of this.

At the beginning of the year, my sister in New Zealand had made a proposal that I simply could not refuse. She asked me to organize US visas and plane tickets to the United States for the entire family because she wanted to treat the children to Disneyland and, further, pay for our accommodations in the US. It was an offer I simply could not resist. Before long, the exciting prospect of our first family US holiday and the kids' first Disneyland experience was part and parcel of our daily family prayers, and we spoke about this consistently in the hope that our finances would catch the vision and rise to the challenge.

I decided not to worry about the money and to focus on working as hard as possible. That way, I was doing my part while fully expecting a miracle, with absolutely no doubt in my mind that I would see one. We searched for flights online and found a few options for March 30, which was also Good Friday.

My busy February turned into an even busier March, with a facilitation opportunity in Mozambique. I looked forward to my out-of-country training trip but grew more and more uneasy as the days drew closer. The end of March was approaching quickly, and the finances for our dream holiday did not seem to be materializing. Although I began to panic and grow anxious, I decided to keep up the faith by encouraging the children to pray earnestly for a miracle. Truth be told, I really had no clue where the kind of money I was expecting would come from, but that really wasn't my problem, and I decided not to worry about it.

Mozambique was a successful work assignment. I enjoyed the group that I worked with, and I met a few other foreigners who were on business in Maputo. Despite all of this, I had a feeling of dread that was growing stronger and stronger each day.

Returning to Johannesburg was hard. My husband picked me up from the airport, and as usual he was his simple, practical self and said nothing about the holiday dream. I expressed to him how much I was dreading seeing the children and having to tell them that the money had not come through for our US dream.

He casually told me that I shouldn't worry about that because he had already managed expectations with the children. He added that they had accepted the fact that it might not happen now. A wave of mixed emotions came over me. One part of me felt an overwhelming sense of relief that I didn't have to be the one to break the awful news. That lasted a brief moment. For the rest of the trip, my mind was a jungle of activity, pondering how much my life had changed since I left full-time employment. I reflected back on the money that I had earned during those years of executive management and how easy it had been to decide upon a holiday, book it, and pay. Now here I was, unable to afford a simple visit to the US and facing the reality of letting my sister down. Periodically, my mind would wander back to the stress of full-time employment and the days, weeks, and months spent rushing about, trying to arrive somewhere in time to collect the children, being late for recitals and concerts, and just feeling plain exhausted. I was too disappointed to care about that for now. What I really needed was another executive job to patch up the gaps we had in our finances and to make sure that this level of disappointment was never experienced by the children again. I really didn't want them to look back on their childhood and remember being let down and never having enough money for holidays.

As I wallowed silently in self-pity, my phone rang, and it was my sister-in-law. She had called to congratulate me on my Mozambique assignment, and she exclaimed, "Wow, Val, you're doing it! Your leaving work was really the right thing for you to do, and it's paying off. I don't think your kids would have come so far if you hadn't done it."

That remark stabbed me in the chest. How was it that I felt so down and disappointed and like a bit of a loser as a parent, and someone else thought I was a hero? I knew all of the theory about what children really needed and that money doesn't buy happiness. But I felt so sore at that time. All I could really do then was sigh—sigh and hope that my aspirations and my reality would someday meet.

My "depression," if I may call it that, lasted longer than I had hoped it would. It felt like a marking point in my year, and I decided to indulge myself in it completely. I was very disappointed, and I wasn't going to pretend otherwise. I had done all I could to try to make this trip happen, and I felt extremely disappointed to say the least. I would go as far as to say that I felt mad and let down, like I was entitled to be mad.

I had no contract work planned for the weeks to follow, so I decided to just sit at home and allow myself to walk through my disappointment until I was done. So I read books, watched television, and did little else. It felt good to be able to do so without feeling guilty. My husband took the liberty of having a frank conversation with me one morning, in which he made it very clear that while he understood my sense of disappointment, nobody owed me anything, and I would benefit from planning and saving up for a holiday rather than trusting for a miracle. The children got over it soon enough, and we had enough local fun outings for them to entirely forget about the US. Soon thereafter, we got the opportunity to go away to our holiday apartment in Durban, which turned out to be just what the doctor had ordered for all four of us. We spent the most relaxing five days by the beach in that small coastal town, sleeping in, taking walks, playing games, and just being us.

Coming back to the big city wasn't as bad as it usually is. We had missed our home and our malls and cosmopolitan environment. And I realized that I was finally healed. I could move on with the rest of the year and focus on growing my business.

The weeks that followed required me to be organized and flexible. A number of facilitation appointments were scattered sporadically on my calendar, which meant from one day to the next, I might be moving from discussing the importance of business etiquette to delving into the science of emotions and their relevance to leadership. No complaints from me. I was more than grateful to have work, which meant bills would be paid, and I could do some grocery shopping at month's end, which was now some sort of rare occurrence.

So I got on with what I did best. I drew up schedules, organized kids' transport, and planned my exercise and driving distances to make sure I rocked up on time and delivered a fair day's work without having to worry about how the children got home. Occasionally, I worked from home, either writing blogs and uploading them or preparing for upcoming training. In between, I began to read again, which was a luxury I had forgotten about since my children were born. Now I found I could actually finish a whole book within the space of a month, and I tried hard not to feel guilty about this luxurious indulging.

As the weeks wore on, I became more and more aware of the gradual decrease in my subcontracting work. One of the projects I had been working on was drawing to a close, and this had been a significant contributor to my monthly earnings since the previous year, so I felt a level of anxiety about this. Steve and I had the occasional talk about finances, and he was very clear that he felt I ought to look for a full-time position in order to help with the growing household finances. I felt awful about the fact that I really didn't want to go back to full-time work. While I agreed with him that we were under tremendous financial pressure, I loathed the thought of having to be anywhere at eight o'clock on a Monday morning, let alone having to stay in one place until 5:00 p.m. So I embarked on even more marketing. I reached out to over 150 people on social media, advertising my services and offering partnerships in delivering training and coaching. Unfortunately, the responses I received were largely polite thank-yous and "we'll keep you in mind" and nothing concrete.

Fortunately, I still had a good amount of facilitation work for the remainder of the month, and I got on with this as dutifully as possible. I also committed myself to blogging and uploading my work on a new blog site with links to social media. Hopefully, potential clients would catch a glimpse of what I could do and contact me.

Despite my attempts, there was silence on all social media platforms, and the phone was hardly ringing. It was about exam time for both children, so I busied myself with helping them prepare for these dreaded appointments. I had a sense of purpose again and enjoyed the time spent with the children during their study week. I decided that I really enjoyed being home, and nothing was going to send me off to full-time work again. If only I could get this business going and create sustainable revenue and contribute to household expenses.

Exams came and went, and the children received good and excellent marks in their various subjects. My husband and I were proud of their efforts, and round about the same time, I reminded him that we had scheduled another Durban holiday and that both children would be off school at the same time, which was now a rare occurrence. He obliged, and before long we were packing up again to go away to the sea.

I prayed that the time away would give me some much-needed inspiration and a plan for how to revive my business. The time in Durban was once again exactly what the doctor had ordered. The weather was at least ten degrees warmer than in Johannesburg, which was a welcome surprise for all four of us. We slept late and woke up no earlier than nine each morning, after spending evenings watching World Cup soccer and playing four-hour-long Monopoly matches. Our little apartment was a stress-free zone, and we basked in the relaxation. No one had any major concerns or occupations, and our mornings were filled with beach walks, laid-back breakfasts indoors, and slow turns in and out of the shower until we were all clean. Thereafter, we would be ushered by the children to some preplanned activity (they had drawn up an entire week's schedule—they learned from the best), and we would spend the day at the movies, embarking on zip-line adventures, watching dolphin shows at Ushaka, or lunching at the mall. This really was the life.

Despite all of the welcome rest and relaxation, I could not help but wonder how we were going to navigate the next few months financially in the absence of sufficient contract work.

I swung in and out of decisions to go back to work or to stay and push my business harder. My going-back-to-work days were focused on the financial rewards of full-time work and how relieving it would be for us to have the additional income and be able to not only meet all of our current financial obligations but even save and invest. What a beautiful dream. On the flip side of that coin, though, I panicked at the thought of having to be somewhere at eight on a Monday morning, stay there until close of business at least, and have someone else decide on my activities via meeting requests and diary entries. I also remembered how much I hated office politics, the idea of not being able to collect the children when they came out of class, and the prospect of giving up managing my own time. I worried about coming home after dark and missing homework time and even supper with the family. The honest truth is that I just plain hated the idea of going back to full-time work.

Speaking to my husband was getting more difficult now that he had clearly expressed his desire regarding my occupational activities. I felt guilty for not wanting to go back to full-time, and although I tried to make him see the benefits of my being more home-based, I hated sounding like I didn't want to help him out. About the same time, a very good old friend of mine came to visit from Namibia. It was a much-needed visit. I basked in the warmth of a friendship that had been birthed more than two decades ago at university. Chengetai probably knew me better than most people, and she had sensed my anxiety about finances. Her very strongly expressed opinion was that I should honor my husband and go back to work. I felt sad to hear this, knowing how much she knew me and cared about the well-being of my marriage. I took her advice seriously and bought a copy of the newspaper to see what jobs awaited me.

Browsing through the paper, I could not help but notice the type of work that was available to me. For the salary range that I had been used to, I was looking at executive-level jobs whose descriptions were exhausting to read, let alone enact. I had visions of my old office. It was a large space filled with a restricting U-shaped desk, an executive leather chair, two visitor chairs, a bookshelf, and—wait for it—a full couch set with coffee table. Not to mention my mini refrigerator! It was draining just to think of the hours I had spent in that office and the numerous times I had looked out the window onto the nearby park, longing to be free. I had wished then that I could be released from the leather prison to collect my children, take them to their extramurals, and play with them!

That dream had come true. Was I now wishing myself back there?

A LITTLE PIECE OF
PARADISE

Many months after my daughter had moved to her new school, I really felt the fundraising bug begin to grow on me. I looked for opportunities to give back, which incidentally was the motto of her school. I guess I felt a sense of obligation to act in line with the school's values since the school had generously provided her with a scholarship for her education.

I came across Paradise Bend Primary School while researching possible beneficiary schools that our school could work with. I really didn't want to partner with a school that was already on the receiving end of a number of partnerships with private schools or investment banks, which I found most common when I began my research. Paradise Bend was a primary school in the Diepsloot informal settlement and apparently had not had any form of support since it was established in the 1960s.

I remember the morning I set aside to visit the school, to investigate the extent of their needs and take a look at what they were working with. I drove around the informal settlement for at least half an hour, lost. The GPS was clearly as lost as I, considering that it continued to issue me impossible instructions to turn left where there was in fact no road. There was one main road in the area, and once you ventured off that road, you were left to your own devices since the dusty foot roads were clearly not recognized by geo-satellite systems.

When I eventually arrived at the school, it was difficult to find anyone with authority to speak to. The headmaster was out of the office, and one or two senior teachers wanted to know the purpose of my visit before they rushed off to teach their classes. Finally, a committed art teacher offered to help and sat me down and schooled me on everything I needed to know about that little paradise of learning in the middle of nowhere. She took me on a mini tour of the school and was excited about my proposal to bring in a group of moms to assist the children with reading. Of course, she verbalized her wish for financial assistance for additional classrooms (they were operating primarily from porter cabins) as well as additional furniture to cater to the overpopulated classrooms. The school tour was heartbreaking. Up to sixty little faces stared up at me in each of the classes, sharing desks and in some cases chairs. What really touched my heart was the joy they seemed to have. Despite their difficult circumstances, they seemed genuinely happy to be at school, which I felt was a great start.

Within a few weeks, I convinced my wonderful teacher friend and a small group of mothers to accompany me on a visit back to the school, and we succeeded in obtaining approval from our school to adopt this precious paradise and launch our reading program. There was some virtue in this life after all.

Once we had established Thursdays as our reading morning with the school, our small group of mothers organized not only to drive together to our paradise school but also to upskill ourselves in how to effectively teach reading to the children.

On the very first reading morning, we had quickly discovered that many of these wonderful children could not read even though they were already in grade 4, and we wondered how they had progressed this far without the essential skill of reading. Even more concerning was the prospect that they might complete their primary schooling and be promoted to high school with a weak reading foundation.

As the months wore on, our group of reading moms looked forward to seeing those bright and excited faces each Thursday morning. We fully understood the level of demotivation that the teachers seemed to have. They were alone at the school (mostly without the presence of the headmaster or other authority), and apart from the lack of equipment and facilities, there was sewage water running across the school campus. In spite of this, we prepared ourselves regularly for our weekly appointment with the children.

It was during our reading sessions that we began to notice that some of these little ones were struggling to see. One little boy had bloodshot eyes week in and week out, and a few others seemed to be squinting to see the words before them.

Fortunately, our Fundraising Queen was quick to approach a local optometrist, who agreed to conduct a visual screening for all two hundred grade 4 learners. It was heartwarming to realize that there were still good people in the world. The visual screening exercise revealed that thirteen learners required thorough eye testing, and approximately twelve needed regular eye exercises.

Our faithful optometrist offered the further tests free of charge, and we were able to organize our school bus to ferry the children to the optometrist. Before long, those learners needing spectacles had received them free of charge, and we had been trained to conduct regular eye exercises with the learners. The little boy with the red eyes was referred to another generous-hearted ophthalmologist, who diagnosed him with conjunctivitis and prescribed medication, which was affordable due to our extensive fundraising activities. My heart was touched deeply by these partnerships. I felt a sense of fulfillment in having had the opportunity to tangibly help these children. They mostly came from communities with a vast number of social ills and families with much dysfunction.

After the eye examinations the optometrist drew my attention to a little girl named Buhle. While conducting Buhle's eye exam, the doctor had discovered that the girl was completely blind in one eye. When the optometrist asked what had happened to her eye, Buhle informed her that a piece of glass had flown into her eye more than five years ago when she was playing with a neighbor. She couldn't remember whether she had ever been taken to see a doctor for her eye, but it turned out that the piece of glass had caused considerable damage to the tissue, resulting in blindness in that eye. Once again, our kind optometrist called in a favor with an eye surgeon, and before long I had been given an appointment for Buhle, free of charge. I began what would turn out to be the long and taxing task of getting hold of Buhle's mom to organize an early morning pickup to take them both to the specialist appointment.

Buhle's class teacher tried repeatedly to reach Buhle's mother. She left voice messages that were never returned, and when we had almost given up hope, the teacher tried one last time and got hold of her. Although Buhle's mother agreed in principle for me to collect her and her daughter, she disappeared again for weeks, and we missed the specialist appointment.

My heart was sore for Buhle. She had had an eye accident early in her childhood, and she couldn't remember whether her family had ever taken this seriously enough to consult a doctor. Now there was a once-in-a-lifetime opportunity to save her sight, and once again it appeared not to be a priority. I vowed not to give up on Buhle. Many times, we had visited the children at this little school and wondered whether we were making a true difference. Now we knew we were.

Buhle's mother eventually surfaced a few months later, and we were able to take Buhle to her eye appointment. The specialist treated her free of charge and offered her an annual checkup to look after her eye right up until she finishes school! There are still good people in the world!

TEA, TALK, AND SCONES

While I was basking in the warm Durban sun, a friend called me up to ask if I could be guest speaker at her women's event. I happily obliged, thinking of it as my debut into women's workshops and learning forums. A couple of days thereafter, I received the invitation she had been circulating and was quite intimidated. It was most beautiful and professional and made me sound somewhat famous. I loved it, though, and chose to view it as a sign of things to come.

The days rolled by, and the day eventually came. As I expected, I fully enjoyed the entire experience, and before I knew it, we had run out of time, and I still had a whole lot to say. Jolly had done an amazing job of setting up the room and catering for the event, and it was an intimate and professional affair. I must have been really inspired by the experience because all I could think of on my way home was that I really wanted to do more of that!

The weather in Johannesburg was icy cold, and I couldn't help but crawl into bed after morning school drop-offs. What a luxury it was to be able to do so. I felt a need to enjoy and savor the time since I wasn't sure how long it would last. I also appreciated the peace and quiet of not having to be stuck in traffic or rushing to get places. This time gave me a chance not only to rest but also to reflect upon what I really wanted and what success would mean for me. Of course, I wanted more money; almost everyone I knew did. But would that be the answer? What effect would my long absences have on the family and the children in particular? Would I still have time for my husband when he came home? And secretly, I had determined in my heart that I would begin my PhD the following year. I had submitted the application online and was awaiting transcript verification. I knew this would require a significant amount of my time, and it was something I was willing to put my time and effort toward without a doubt. I felt somewhat selfish for wanting to do this (which required money—lots of it) rather than go off to work to generate money.

The conversations at the morning workshop had been intriguing. For the longest time I had felt quite alone in my determination not to go back to full-time work, and here were a good number of ladies who had walked down the exact same road. They shared stories with me of how they had left the corporate world and either started a business or simply waited until they had fully recovered from the trauma of senior management in corporate and state-owned entities. We laughed at situations that would have been very serious and stressful at the time and wondered how we had in fact survived the frequent traveling, the running late for aftercare, and the speeding down the highway, trying to make it to a child's piano lesson or concert on time. We gasped at the trauma of painful board meetings, of being ostracized for trying by all means to do the right thing, and of the vindictive payback tactics of colleagues and managers who didn't appreciate what we stood for. We had survived it all. The experience felt like soldiers getting together after war. There were wounds that ran deep, some of which would take years to heal, but the peace that came with standing up for the right thing could not be undermined. I wasn't alone in the world. We even laughed at the reactions of husbands who'd had to live with us during these tumultuous times, about their rapid acclimatization to increased household income and the sluggish and painful reality of the end of the season of milk and honey. It was comforting to know that it really wasn't just me, and I was able to laugh at the days gone by.

As the days and weeks wore on, the radio waves were abuzz with news of an impending recession, and I began to notice how quiet my phone had become. In previous months, I had begun to choose the type of work that I did because I was presented with multiple offers of training work from different agencies. Lately, however, the phone was just not ringing, and I earnestly spent that quiet time preparing my own courses and investigating options for office space.

Interestingly, when I began to talk about the business I was building, I found that many of the mothers in my school community (including some of my reading moms) were busy setting up businesses of their own. We exchanged information on registering and setting up companies, and I learned of a relatively new entrepreneurial hub that was situated a few minutes from my children's schools. I was most amazed at how much was out there as well as how much I began to learn once I started talking to other women like myself. I really wasn't alone, and many of the women who I had mistakenly thought were living off a gigantic inheritance in fact either were building new businesses or had been running their own enterprises for years.

I intensified my efforts toward growing my business and applied for office space. I could feel the wind in my sails again and had a new determination to succeed in business. I started calling prospective clients again, reminding them that I was still here and that I was available to work.

I was amazed at the impact a cup of tea and scones could have on a business.

CHASING BUSINESS
(UP AND DOWN COUNTRY)

Within days of what seemed to be my "desperate" season, I received a call from an agent with a bank coaching project that would take place at various business locations across the country. Of course, I jumped at the opportunity! At this stage I really didn't mind if they sent me to Timbuktu. As long as it was work that I could do, and it paid, I was game.

So within weeks I had my bags packed and was off. The project took me to a few different provinces, and this meant full weeks away from home. My husband thought I was becoming a migrant worker, and I felt like I was in boarding school. On Sunday I would get that feeling of dread about my own impending departure, and I felt very envious of the rest of the family, who had the good fortune of staying together the entire week. I breathed a sigh of relief that our son was staying in his current school for high school as opposed to the all-boys boarding school that we initially had thought was a great idea. It would have made me very sad to have him go through what I was going through, but of course, he is young and resilient, so it's possible that he would have absolutely loved boarding school. Well, I was just thankful that we would still have the privilege of living with him and enjoying his sense of humor!

And so the long-distance drives began. I must confess that I had been terribly spoiled by my husband, who never let me drive long distances. Whenever we took family holidays, he did all of the driving, and my sole duty was to sit on the passenger seat and look pretty.

Now here I was, having to drive up to 450 kilometers from home at a time, alone in a hired vehicle. As if that wasn't bad enough, the company was not about to pay for automatic-transmission cars, so it was back to the clutch and gear-shifting, which resulted in stiff and achy forty-year-old knees!

The view of the countryside made up for the driving exhaustion. What lovely landscapes that I had never seen before. The long drives gave me plenty of time to reflect on my life, on where I had come from and where I was going. It was already October, and the year had seemed to just fly by. My business had grown somewhat, and even though I sometimes felt like I was making no money at all, a quick calculation done for tax purposes had shown me otherwise. It was clear that things were improving. Financially, we were nowhere near where we had been in my corporate years, but there had been significant progress from the previous year. So somewhere during the busyness of the activities, things were indeed getting better. I felt encouraged and hopeful.

Staying in guesthouses was an experience that I had to stomach and that I hope I do not have to repeat too frequently. I really struggled with the idea of staying in a stranger's home. I can live with hotels because they were built for the sole purpose of housing paying strangers. However, most of the bed-and-breakfasts I stayed in had initially been people's homes, and over time children had grown up and left, or a wife or husband had passed away, leaving a lone widow or widower needing to earn a living. And my anxiety about cleanliness certainly didn't help the situation. Yes, it's amazing how moving from your home environment places a huge spotlight on these tendencies! I struggled with the fact that I couldn't touch door handles, flush toilets, or turn taps without first sterilizing everything. I couldn't use the crockery and cutlery in my room, which I was sure had been washed in the toilet sink and dried with a dirty cloth that had been used a thousand times on other not-so-clean items. So I quickly became accustomed to carrying around my own dishwashing liquid and sponge and my own coffee mug, spoon, and fork. What a mission!

I don't actually remember when I became so obsessed with cleanliness, but I have clear recollections of the not-so-clean cutlery we used in the dining room at university decades ago and how my friend and I got into the habit of polishing our forks and knives thoroughly with serviettes before eating.

All in all, it was rather exhausting, and on more than one of those trips, I ended up going to the local grocery store and purchasing my own utensils and plastic containers. I guess this is one of those things that worsen as we grow older, and I have become a bit more anxious than before.

The weeks on the road were a great opportunity for me to recognize the privilege I enjoyed in my day-to-day life. I thought about the number of people, particularly women, who did this much traveling and specifically driving every week of their lives for a living. I considered the salespeople and business executives who had to go for days on end without seeing their families and without a home-cooked meal. I had lain down to sleep in so many different locations and different beds that I had lost count. Whenever I arrived in a new location, I didn't have the luxury of days to settle into my new temporary home. I had to simply unpack and get on with life, grin and bear whatever meal was served to me, and focus on the real purpose of my travels. And invariably, every time, there was a new set of faces waiting for me whenever I arrived at the client's office. They didn't know who I was, and the same was true from my end. And we didn't have much time to get to know each other and work together. I was in and out of each corporate office and had the privilege of meeting scores of employees and managers and getting a snapshot of their day-to-day responsibilities as I coached them.

All over the country, it seemed to be the same story—men and women trying the best way they knew how to make the best of difficult work and/or personal circumstances. I met bank branch managers who were full-on professional people, highly competent and motivated and stuck in a town that many of us would call "the middle of nowhere" in a flash. I met mothers who had moved to particular towns in pursuit of a better life because the job had required them to relocate, and they bitterly missed their children, who were often in the capable hands of their mothers in remote villages.

One woman I will never forget burst into tears during her coaching session as she apologized for being somewhat emotional because today was the anniversary of her husband's death. They had been together for eighteen years when he had died suddenly a year ago, leaving her with a whole church congregation to pastor and two children who desperately missed their father.

Suddenly, I felt really grateful for my own life. I was sorry for the times I had moaned and complained, wishing my circumstances could be better. Now more than ever, I was grateful for my family, my life, and my home, grateful that I did not need to move miles away from my children in order to provide for them, and grateful for my husband. I was grateful that my work did not always require me to drive long, hot distances to the middle of nowhere, leaving every Monday morning and returning home on Friday nights. I was grateful for being able to live in my own home, for being able to choose what food I ate, and for the privilege of living in a city with proper water and sanitation services, electricity (most of time), and shopping malls that provided me with a choice of goods and prices.

My great road trip ended in a very small town on the border of two provinces. As small as it was, I had two clients in that town, and on the final day of training, I arrived at the branch with my car fully loaded with my bags, ready to head for home once the day was done.

The morning got off to a smooth start, and I felt a slight attachment to the little town as I walked over to the supermarket to purchase a bottle of water. Everyone seemed to know each other, and I had been greeted with suspicion when I had arrived a few days earlier. I was an unusual face, and many wanted to know who I was and what I was doing there. After day one, I had become part of the furniture, and the small town had continued with its long, slow business days and a lot of foot traffic as pedestrians frequented retail stores and swarmed in and out of the supermarket. Before long, my final workday there was done, and I bade farewell to the staff in the client's office. They had become accustomed to the slow pace of life and business in the small town and were content to fill up their time surfing the internet and communicating on social media.

As I pulled out of my parking space, I switched on my satellite navigation and cranked the air conditioner to maximum. It was a scorching 34 degrees Celsius outside. I was heading home now, and according to the GPS, it would take me less than four hours to get there. As I approached the unsophisticated highway, I relaxed into the driver's seat and prepared to steadily engage the car at a consistent speed. There were a number of other vehicles on the highway, and I gave them way as I was in no particular rush. I was determined to get home safely and free of traffic fines.

It wasn't long before our steady flow seemed to get slower and slower, until we reached a complete standstill. I was surprised by the volume of traffic on this stretch of road because I had not considered it a busy road in the least. Within minutes the cause of our backup became crystal clear. As a long-haul truck made a U-turn in front of me, I could see them: a group of young boys clad in political party T-shirts in the middle of the road. Each of them was carrying one or two small rocks in hand and stoning any cars that dared drive past. This was the sort of scene I had read of in newspapers and heard of frequently on the radio, but never in my life had I actually encountered one. I stepped on my brakes as my mind raced. I didn't have much time to decide on my course of action, and my next action took me completely by surprise. As a number of vehicles made their U-turns back to where we had come from, my head seemed inundated with facts and points to consider. We had already driven a good forty-five minutes to get here, and going back would mean taking a longer route home, which would mean delaying my arrival time by at least a couple of hours. At the same time, the voice of reason whispered to me that I would be endangering my life by proceeding, that I would be risking damage to my hired vehicle, and that there was no guarantee that another group of boys was not lying in wait further up the road. In my flurry of thoughts and panic, what happened next surprised me as much as it probably surprised the car behind me. My foot swiftly moved from the brake pedal to the accelerator, and with my shoulders hunched into a semi-ducking position, I sped past the youths, missing a shower of flying missiles.

Within minutes I was in what appeared to be the clear, and as my heart thumped inside my chest, I looked in my rearview mirror to check that they were not pursuing me. As I looked, I noticed that the driver of the car that had been behind me had taken courage from my bravado and was hot on my heels. I silently prayed that there wasn't another group waiting for me further up the road, and thankfully, there wasn't. The next stretch of road ran along a beautiful winding mountainside, with the most breathtaking view of lush green farms deep within the valley below. I breathed a sigh of relief as I proceeded with my long journey home. The events of that day seemed to be a fitting way to end an adventurous season of business up and down country.

SIX GROUNDING WEEKS

I had not been back home a week when it was time to welcome my parents to Johannesburg. They had both come for medical checkups, and my father in particular urgently needed to see a specialist about his eye, which had been worrying him for some time. He had been to see an optician in Zimbabwe who had assured him that his eyesight was fantastic, but he wasn't convinced.

My parents' arrival signaled a slowing-down season for me. I knew I would be busy taking them to and from their doctors' appointments, so I made sure everything was scheduled within the first week to allow time for any additional tests or requirements thereafter. I had a number of training courses lined up for the end of October and November, but the scheduling gave me a sense of structure and control that was much needed.

The appointments with the general practitioner went as expected, with no surprises. As usual, our GP was fantastic. The doctor treated both my parents with the utmost respect and was extremely thorough, providing holistic and complementary recommendations for their many conditions. It seemed that at their age a lot was beginning to either malfunction or visibly deteriorate in their bodies. I felt a sense of compassion for them and became sharply aware that they were no longer able to do things as quickly as before and that I needed to exercise patience. I was grateful for this too. It always helps to get some insight into seasons to come and, I guess, to be better prepared. Both my parents had remained very active both physically and mentally and were very fit for their ages. Unfortunately, the medical support in Zimbabwe ranged from little to nonexistent, and when it was available, it was limited to those with large sums of US dollars.

The visit to the optician left me feeling somewhat mad. As the competent young optometrist chatted to me about my father's vision (or rather lack thereof) in the right eye, I could not reconcile what she was reporting with what he had been told by the optometrist in Zimbabwe. She quickly explained to me that the superb report he had received in Zimbabwe was likely due to a lack of equipment, and my father concurred that only a small fraction of the tests had actually been conducted for that very reason. I was incredulous but thankful that South Africa still provided hope for the region.

Dad's diagnosis warranted an immediate appointment with an ophthalmologist, which was facilitated by the kind young optometrist. To cut a long story short, the ophthalmologist confirmed the report and actually presented a grimmer picture. He took me aside to explain that my dad had an actual hole in his eye and had lost almost 80 percent vision in that eye. He warned that this would likely worsen if my dad did not receive immediate surgery. Again, the doctor was kind enough to facilitate a quick appointment with a retina specialist in the area, and my brother took Dad in for the appointment. I was driving home from a meeting that afternoon when I heard the ping of text message alerts on my cell phone. My brother had sent several messages, including voice notes, detailing the findings of the retina specialist as well as the quote that he had been provided for the surgery.

R50,000! That was the quote my brother had been given for Dad's surgery. I drove home in silence, knowing that somehow that money needed to be found. After everything that Dad and

Mom had done for all of us growing up, there was no way that any of us would let R50,000 stand between Dad and full sight.

Fortunately, the surgeon offered to give us a discount, and R38,000 and four days later, Dad was sitting on the surgeon's chair, having his sight-saving surgery. We were all very grateful when he came out of what seemed to have been successful surgery. Dad had been ordered to keep his head down for four days thereafter, and he was happy to do this, knowing that it would help to save his sight.

Thankfully, Dad's surgery was declared successful when he went in for his follow-up appointment. A condition of the surgery was that he could not fly for one month thereafter. As such, my parents had to extend their stay for another four weeks, giving them a full six-week vacation from the stressful life that they had grown accustomed to in Zimbabwe. It felt as though we all decided to settle and calm down once we knew they were around for longer. There was no longer a pressing sense of urgency about what needed to be done before their departure, and they began to settle into life in Johannesburg.

They held some very interesting views on life in Johannesburg, particularly my mother, who periodically remarked at the fast pace of life and compared it to the one that she had lived while we were growing up. She could not believe the extent of back-and-forth travel involved in one single day and the number of responsibilities that came with parenting, running a business, and running a household. She made me long for a slower life, and I regularly daydreamed of a miraculous turnaround in the Zimbabwean economy and of us moving the entire family there and living the African dream in a quiet, leafy Harare suburb with access to the country's top schools and regular holidays to Cape Town! That would certainly be the life.

Dad was less vocal about the pace of life in Johannesburg. Instead he kept reminding us of the tremendous opportunity that was available to us. He reminisced on the state of the

Zimbabwean economy years ago and expressed disbelief at the glaring contrasts between life then and now. He warned us of the dangers of relying on an income and pension and encouraged us to explore as many entrepreneurial opportunities as possible. Experience had taught him never to trust the government system that promised to look after citizens into their old age, but he and all his former colleagues had received a laughable pittance of a pension as the Zimbabwe dollar had crashed into oblivion and left the pensioners without a pension and the youth without any hope for jobs. I counted my blessings as I heard of the true state of my country. I had actually never worked in Zimbabwe. After my studies I had been fortunate enough to get a job and a work permit in South Africa and had escaped the woes of having to survive in the difficult Zimbabwean economy.

The month was a quiet one for me business-wise, and I was grateful for the time to sit and have breakfast with Mom and Dad in the morning and listen to their stories, many of which I had forgotten or had very sketchy details around. It was amazing to put together the pieces of the puzzle. It felt as though I had gaps all over, some of which I had filled with half-true information. Others were just plain gaps in my memories of people, events, and places.

Upon my sister's request, I began to put together a family tree to document our history, and that was an interesting exercise to say the least. Both my parents retold stories and events when they reflected upon who was who. They also appeared to have gaps in their memories of people, but they helped each other remember the connections. The years seemed to be the least clear in their memories. Was that uncle born in 1955, or was it more like 1958? Who was older, him or his sister? Did that cousin remarry after running away from her husband and children in 1973? It sounded like a book of African stories. With the memory of each person and their relationship to each of my parents came a story or an event that enriched my own understanding of who I was and where I had come from.

In the midst of this exciting exercise, it emerged that my mother came from a lineage of artists, with her own mom having been a strong vocal student and lifelong member of the church choir. Her uncle had been a musician who played the accordion, and his daughter was currently a vocal artist who regularly performed in Johannesburg. My mother was still very proud of the fact that she had been awarded an art scholarship to New Zealand in the 1970s; only the small matter of a passport (the lack thereof) had prevented her from taking up the opportunity. All the pieces really were coming together. Both my children are passionate all-round musicians, and my niece is a fantastic artist. Finally, all the dots were connecting in a beautiful way.

I listened with compassion as my father retold the few stories he could remember of his own mother and father. He had been orphaned at a very young age and had lost his mother first, at the age of ten. He told of the number of afternoons he had played outside the hut, looking into the sunset and imagining he could see his mother approaching with a pile of wood on her head. At the age of ten, it must have been a painful experience to repeatedly stare into the distance with a longing for his mother, only to realize that it was a figment of his imagination and that his mother was not coming back. He told of the experience of having to go and live with his uncle after his mother passed away and how his uncle's wife, who had clearly had no say in the matter, had struggled to accept the additional responsibility.

I felt a dull pain on hearing these things. My father had truly lived as an orphan and still remembered the feeling of being excluded or kept on the periphery of family life. It all began to make sense to me. I remember the anger I felt, growing up, at his overstated sense of responsibility for any and every child who was struggling or in need and at how so many of these very needy ones had taken full advantage of my parents' kindness and even abused my parents. It was difficult to reconcile these very different experiences with the life that we were living in

Johannesburg. A life where our own needs were at the center of the universe, and we didn't even know the names of the people next door or in the house across the road from us. How vastly different was the life he was describing from the life in which my children did not know all of their cousins or even their names and vice versa. And what shall we say to Dad's philosophy when today we are taught to establish and manage boundaries and to understand the extent and reach of our responsibility and distinguish this from what is not our responsibility?

And there was Mom. Although her mother had lived well into her sixties, she had not lived with her for very long. Mom's dad passed away very early in Mom's life, and as if that wasn't bad enough, her beloved older brother went off to fight in the war for freedom, never to be seen again. The two of them had shared both parents and had been very close growing up. After her father's death and her brother's disappearance, Mom had been bused off to the village to be raised by her maternal grandmother, along with four other cousins who later become like sisters to her. As I worked on the family tree, I could see the deep emotions that the exercise brought about for my mother. Her mother had remarried, and her half sisters had brought Mom a considerable amount of stress after my grandmother died, as they had fought my mom, who had power of attorney over my grandmother's property. I had to choose whether to argue with Mom over the importance of accuracy and factuality in a family tree or to respect her desire for peace. I chose the latter.

Working from home and getting on with my day-to-day routine with Mom and Dad in the house made me feel a bit like I was back home again. They seemed to calmly observe my behaviors and mostly did not comment on how I ran things. My father, being very observant, asked me a few questions about how I was running my business—simple questions about tax, billing, and whether I was charging my clients for all the extras that I was putting into my delivery such as printing, fuel, and telephone calls. It wasn't that I hadn't thought of these things, but the honest truth is that I was caught between feeling bad for charging for them and being somewhat too lazy to actually record these matters for tax purposes. I felt like I had been cheating myself out of running a more professional business. Suddenly, I had a heightened desire to make the most of the business I had. My parents were both so interested in what I was doing that they took turns reading through a proposal I was due to submit to a multinational for coaching. I really had never thought they would care that much, but they proved me wrong. Even in my forties, when I should have been big enough to handle my own business and just get on with it, I was appreciative of their interest in my life. Living in Johannesburg, I had learned that no one had the time to do things like this for others and that I had to comb through my work myself, enough times to make sure that it was seamless. I basked in this newfound attention. Being a mom, a wife, a business owner, and a self-boss, I really couldn't remember when I had received this much attention and support. Support had always been my job to provide rather than to receive.

Surrounded by this newfound reinforcement, I took the liberty of opening up for discussion the possibility of my going back to a full-time permanent job. For months now I had been bothered as I looked around at other families who seemed to have it more together than I did. Working moms were able to contribute a reliable income to the household that enabled their families to go on well-planned holidays that did not run the risk of being canceled in the eleventh hour, as had already happened for us earlier in the year. Their children wore quality clothing and enjoyed gadgets galore. I felt as though I was the mom of faith, the one who encouraged her children to have faith and trust for things but with very little substance to show for it. I felt sorry for my children in a strange sort of way. While they were content and cheerful (most of the time), I couldn't help but notice that they wanted what their friends had: holidays in Mauritius, trips to Disney World, and the thrill (albeit temporary) of driving the latest-model cars and owning a drone years before they were available to corporates in our country!

All of these emotions kept me wondering whether it wasn't time to throw in the towel on my business and go back to work. After all, I had given it my best shot. I was hardworking and never said no to work. Most of my work was subcontracted, and I was becoming known for delivery, value, and quality. But financially, I was nowhere near where I had been when I was permanently employed in the corporate world.

To my utmost surprise, neither of my parents was a strong proponent of my idea of going back to work. I'm not sure whether I was more shocked at my father's position or my mother's, but both of them gave me nothing that I expected. My father was a serious advocate for education, and my entire life, he had lectured us regularly on the role that education would play in our ability to function in society, enjoy life, and help others. I remember the lectures prior to the first day of school that took place in the evening after supper, before he retired to bed. He would begin the lecture by reminding us of his own upbringing, which had involved him walking a very lengthy distance from his village to the nearest school, with no shoes. He would then draw our attention to the privilege that we had as children living in the city and attending some of the best schools the country had to offer. The opportunity was there for the taking, and those who were willing would take hold of it with both hands and run with it. He had been very supportive of me when I received my promotion to the executive level a few years ago and had encouraged me to keep striving for excellence and to buy property with the money I earned. So I was rather surprised when he remarked that he felt I ought to give the business a fair chance because "it takes years to build a successful business."

My mother had been very proud of my progress in the workplace, particularly with my advancement to the executive level. She had shared countless photos and held bragging rights over these. When I had made the decision to leave my permanent work, she had been very concerned for our financial wellness, and then when we actually went through hard times financially, she had always been the first to suggest that I call up my old boss and get my job back. She was also very good at reminding me how well I had looked after her and Dad when I was working, and this had been a source of regret for me over the years since I started up my business. Now here she was expressing concern over my desire to go back to work. She told me that she felt that I was growing in my profession as a result of the diverse set of skills that I was developing in consulting and that I ought to give my business some time to grow.

I really didn't know what to think, but I felt a sense of relief. I loved working for myself, even though I felt that I needed a more professional space from which to do it. I also realized the gaps that existed in my business that I had to work hard to close. What I really took away from my parents' views on the subject was that they approved of me. They were proud of me and everything I was working toward, and they had faith that I could grow it.

That was all I needed.

SAYING GOODBYE TO AN ERA

So here we are at the end of 2018. What a year it has been! In fact, what a unique two years I have had. Looking back, I never could have guessed what 2017 and 2018 had in store, not in a million years. I spent more time at home in both of these years than over the past fifteen years. For the longest time it felt as though my life was a bit of a treadmill, just going, going, and going, and suddenly in 2017, I was home with very little to do and longing for something to occupy my time. The year 2018 was not as quiet as the prior year, but I desperately wanted my business to grow. I longed for the financial resources that held the potential to change my life and the lives of my family members. But amid the tears, the sense of helplessness, and the quiet moments of feeling alone and lost, there were some very important life lessons.

Probably the most difficult and most painful lesson I learned was that I really was not owed anything. I will never forget my husband telling me this in the most detached and unemotional tone as I coldly faced the reality regarding the trip to the US that never was.

It's strange how I had lived my life right up to midlife with the full expectation that if I hoped enough and held on to my hopes, all of my desires would automatically come to fruition because I believed. I guess I had never really had to face true disappointment, and this was my turn. Just because I had wanted it so much and had dreamed of it and even talked and prayed for it didn't mean that now was the time. It seemed not to matter how much I prayed over and over that it would happen now or how much I cried and spoke to sympathetic friends and family members. When the time is not right, the time is not right. No amount of tears, misery, or longing was going to make it happen at that time. It took some growing up to accept that.

I guess I was left with the option of either concluding that life is unfair and unkind or simply moving on in the knowledge that nothing is guaranteed on this side of eternity, and we need to make the best of what we are given. I've decided to choose the latter. And how ashamed I feel whenever I want to throw a pity party for poor old me. I simply have to think back on the reality of those precious children in Paradise whose best chance lies in their ability to absorb as much as they can in a class with fifty-seven other children and a single teacher battling to connect with each learner. Or I can think back upon an employee whose husband's sudden death left her with a son and daughter to parent on her own, a full-time bank job, and a church to pastor solo, in a community with pronounced gender inequality. Or further still, I may reflect upon the woman who leaves home at the crack of dawn each Monday morning to spend her working week on the road visiting clients as she drives from town to town, with no prospects of seeing her loved ones until the week (and sometimes even the month) is over.

I've always enjoyed escorting my children to their extramural activities, particularly drama and music lessons. I discovered that I not only found the lessons stimulating but also was able to support the children when they practiced for their performances at eisteddfods and other competitions. One of the key lessons they were taught early in their drama years was to use the whole stage and make their actions bigger. I was always the first to remind them of this as I watched them practice or perform, and I went to great lengths to emphasize the point. Looking over my own life, I felt a sense of shame as I admitted that I had not always used the whole stage or owned my space. My halftime reflection had given me a chance to think about how I came across in my own circles to strangers and potential business partners or friends. Why was I limiting my movements to one corner of the stage, and why was I afraid of owning the space available to me? I knew I was doing and feeling these things because of the type of people I met and admired. They all seemed to have the same traits, and they were ambitious go-getters like I was, but they had what I was lacking. They were willing to take up as much space as was needed and make their actions as big as possible.

Being analytical, I began to question why I was this way and what I was afraid of. I could identify endless opportunities that I had had, and while I had gone for them, my default approach had been to go in small and hope that no one noticed my ambition. I recalled that a former manager of mine had commented on this over a decade ago. She was in conversation with a manager from another department, who seemed to have summed me up as rather quiet and harmless. My manager at the time had jumped in (rather quickly, I might add) to advise her colleague not to underestimate me because I held some very strong views, which she had seen me express a few times. I remember feeling rather embarrassed at the thought that I was being described as "strong." I pondered over this and how it might be affecting my life and my business efforts. There was an air of false humility in it that I found repulsive. In essence, I knew I was highly talented and productive but was shying away from attention. I was crying out to be noticed through yelling, "Don't look at me!" After some further introspection and reflection, I believe I learned the motivation behind the "use the whole stage" and "make your actions bigger" motto. The greatest waste in life is to have a beautiful, well-thought-out, precisely practiced performance that no one else has the privilege of seeing and appreciating. The children's teacher had told them that they were stealing from the audience when they did this. I had been doing the same thing by working hard at my skills and expertise and hiding them from the world.

Hanging out with Mom and Dad was an appointment I never would have preempted in a million years. I mean, how many forty-plus-year-olds do you know who get to spend six whole uninterrupted weeks with both their parents in the luxury of their own home? The wealth of wisdom was almost tangible for me, and I soon cultivated the habit of asking myself how they would consider and perceive a situation before I went to them with it. As I mentioned before, it's most useful to get a sneak preview of the seasons to come. It gave me a real sense of being mortal again and an appreciation that I would probably never look and feel this young and energetic again. I vowed to make the most of the time and energy I have now. And that wisdom seems to be accompanied by an eternal lens that presents a perspective that is (more often than not) neither common nor welcome. It's the type of wisdom that makes one ask really deep, thought-provoking questions, like what impact will this have on my life and on my family's life two years from now? You know what I'm talking about. Think about when you've decided to have a small family braai with your nearest and dearest, and you feel that nagging pressure to invite someone who might benefit from inclusion or just exposure to one or two people in your circle. You really will not benefit from it—in fact, more often than not, including them may be a downright pain—but you know it will matter in two years, and if truth be told, it may be their saving grace.

I was proud to be my parents' daughter. Mostly, being out and about with them left me incredulous at the amount of influence they had in their day-to-day encounters with people. Because I am an introvert, my default position is to keep to myself as much as possible, mind my own business, and get on with the purpose of my outing, wherever I am. Mom and Dad, on the other hand, were fully present wherever they were. I recall trips to the doctors' room that led to Dad striking up a conversation with another pensioner and very hearty laughter erupting soon thereafter. Mom had a similar effect on people and made friends with another retiree in a shoe shop. They exchanged notes on foot comfort, and her newfound friend advised on the best shoes and shared stories of how she had worn them in England while visiting her grandchildren. It just seemed that wherever these two went, they brought joy and laughter to people. We could be in a packed elevator, and they had just the thing to say to initiate conversation with a very serious-looking, prefer-to-keep-to-myself-type stranger. My experience of Johannesburg was so different when I was with them. They mattered to people every day of their lives. Perhaps you really do only get what you give.

The weekend after I bade farewell to my parents, I had a long breakfast with one of my friends whom I had not spent time with in months. She had recently completed her master's degree amid parenting four children, working as a home-school teacher, and doing everything else involved with running a functional household. After a relaxed and lengthy brunch, we said our goodbyes, and I remembered that there was a well-known wig shop in the area. I felt a sense of freedom as I jumped into my car and programmed the navigation system to take me there. The forties had hit, and I was feeling like I really needed a new look. Wigs were definitely in, and I had seen hundreds of women like myself sporting the most beautiful wigs, so buying a nice wig had definitely been on my to-do list for a couple of months. The time seemed right, and I had a bit of extra cash, so I felt uplifted as I parked my car outside the upmarket shop and walked into what seemed to be wig heaven, filled with women longing for transformation.

As I walked into the shop, I was immediately greeted by a young man who asked me how he could help me. I told him I wanted to experiment with a new look and try a long shoulder-length wig. He took me around the shop, pointing out the different types of wigs, brands, and prices. The variety was vast, and I really didn't know where to begin. I felt a mixture of excitement and nervousness because I had never really worn a wig before and was keen to see what I would look like. After the salesman gave me a few pieces to try on, I stood in front of the mirror, tilting my head from left to right as I looked at the woman staring back at me with long, flowy hair. I had company. My enthusiastic salesman was also tilting his head from left to right, saying nothing. I felt awkward and thought he needed a course in selling. His job was to give me feedback on what worked and what didn't and to ensure that I walked out of that shop having spent a healthy amount, donned in a wig.

Finally, he spoke. "Why do you want a wig?"

I had to ask him to repeat his question because I was pretty sure that wasn't what he meant to ask me. "Why do I want a wig?"

"Yes."

"Um, because I want to try a new look," I answered uncomfortably. This guy desperately needed to go for sales training.

I was completely unprepared for his response. "Well, you don't need one," he said.

Okay, this was it—he didn't really work there. He was probably one of those guys who hang around women's shops and departments, lying in wait to pounce and strike up unwelcome conversation with unsuspecting women. I laughed out loud. "You're joking, right?" I was sure my retort would awaken him to the reality that he was being paid to interest me in a wig and tell me how fantastic I looked before I paid for it and left.

He seemed more serious than before. "No, I'm serious. You don't need a wig, and I'm wondering why you think you need one."

Okay, this guy was verging on offensive now, and I wondered where the manager was at that point. I could not have predicted what happened immediately thereafter. He asked me to walk toward a mirror in the center of the shop, and then he had the nerve to ask me what I saw. By now I was completed flabbergasted. The one time that I set out to buy a wig, which was something I really had not done before, and I had to get this guy. To cut a long story short, the outspoken salesman proceeded to tell me that what he saw in that mirror was a "confident, motivational community-builder" (his words, not mine) and that I did not need a wig.

I'm not sure if I eventually walked out of that shop because I believed him or because I was simply sick and tired of trying to buy a wig that no one would sell me, but I walked out, got into my car, and drove home. Driving home, I felt a weight lifting from my shoulders, and I breathed a sigh of relief. The encounter at the wig shop had been positively peculiar, but something had happened inside of me. As I walked into the house, I stopped at a full-length mirror and took a long, hard look. I had been reminded of who I was. I love my natural hair and feel most relaxed when I'm in my own hair. I have nothing against wigs—in fact, I still love the idea of them. But what had happened today was confirmation for me. I needed to trust myself a lot more.

This stranger today did not know me from a bar of soap. After he had spent the day selling scores of wigs to scores of women in the shop, he had been bold enough to tell me that he felt that I specifically did not need a wig. He had actually apologized profusely as I was leaving the shop, and by that point, even I knew I didn't need a wig.

The lesson for me that day was to trust my own instincts even more, and finally, after my husband had spent decades repeating these words, I believed them: I was enough.

Printed in the United States
by Baker & Taylor Publisher Services